The Writer's Diet

Chicago Guides
to *Writing*, **Editing**
and Publishing

# The Writer's Diet

*A Guide to Fit Prose*

# Helen Sword

THE UNIVERSITY OF CHICAGO PRESS

*Chicago and London*

HELEN SWORD is professor and director of the Centre for Learning and Research in Higher Education at the University of Auckland. Her books include *Engendering Inspiration, Ghostwriting Modernism, Pacific Rim Modernisms,* and *Stylish Academic Writing*. She also manages the website www.writersdiet.com.

The University of Chicago Press, Chicago 60637
The University of Chicago Press, Ltd., London
© Helen Sword, 2007, 2016
All rights reserved. Published 2016.
Printed in the United States of America

First published by Auckland University Press, 2007
The moral rights of the author have been asserted

25 24 23 22 21 20 19 18     3 4 5

ISBN-13: 978-0-226-35198-8 (PAPER)
ISBN-13: 978-0-226-35203-9 (E-BOOK)
DOI: 10.7208/chicago/9780226352039.001.0001

LIBRARY OF CONGRESS CATALOGING-IN-PUBLICATION DATA
Sword, Helen, author.
　The writer's diet : a guide to fit prose / Helen Sword.
　　pages cm — (Chicago guides to writing, editing, and publishing)
　"First published by Auckland University Press, 2007."—Title page verso.
　ISBN 978-0-226-35198-8 (paperback : alkaline paper) — ISBN 978-0-226-35203-9
(e-book) 1. English language—Rhetoric. 2. English language—Written English. 3.
English language—Style. 4. English language—Style—Problems, exercises, etc. I. Title.
II. Series: Chicago guides to writing, editing, and publishing.
　PE1408.S79 2016
　808'.042—dc23

2015031813

♾ This paper meets the requirements of ANSI/NISO Z39.48-1992
(Permanence of Paper).

# Contents

## ACKNOWLEDGMENTS

We expect a diet guru to be svelte, a personal trainer to sport strong muscles and the author of a book called *The Writer's Diet* to produce flawless prose. In anticipation of robust critique from literary stylists, linguists and grammarians, I invited a number of people to read early drafts of this book and to cast stones both large and small. I thank these generous friends and colleagues by name in the first edition, and I renew my gratitude here.

My writing remains a glass house, of course; but I no longer fear shattered windows. Since its first publication in 2007, readers have embraced *The Writer's Diet*. Some, predictably, have attacked the diet/edit analogy and questioned my fitness algorithms. Most, however, have responded exactly as I hoped they would: with a sense of humor and a grain of salt. A full list of the many people who have sent me helpful feedback about the book and website would fill several pages. I thank them all warmly.

Special thanks to Rachel Booth for early inspiration; to Lois Van Waardenburg for enduring wisdom; to Bronwen Nicholson at Pearson Education New Zealand for her act of faith in publishing the first edition; to Sam Elworthy, Anna Hodge and Katrina Duncan at Auckland University Press, and to Mary Laur and Logan Ryan Smith at the University of Chicago Press for guiding this new version into print; to Gideon Keith for his striking cover design; to John Hamer for bringing the WritersDiet Test to life online; and to Richard, Claire, Peter and David – yes, and Lyra too – for keeping me fit and well-nourished in all the ways that matter most.

# INTRODUCTION: THE WRITER'S DIET

Imagine yourself recruiting a long-distance runner to deliver an important message. What kind of person will you choose: a lean, strong athlete with well-toned muscles and powerful lungs, or a pudgy, unfit couch potato who will wheeze and pant up the first few hills before collapsing in exhaustion? The answer is obvious. Yet far too many writers send their best ideas out into the world on brittle-boned sentences weighted down with rhetorical flab.

This book will help you energize your writing, boost your verbal fitness and strip unnecessary padding from your prose. But whereas a successful exercise regime typically requires weeks or months of sustained effort before you see tangible results, here you will learn how to strengthen and tone your sentences with the stroke of a pen or the click of a mouse. The rules are deceptively simple: use active verbs whenever possible; favor concrete language over vague abstractions; avoid long strings of prepositional phrases; employ adjectives and adverbs only when they contribute something new to the meaning of a sentence; and finally, reduce your dependence on four pernicious "waste words": *it*, *this*, *that* and *there*.

As with any fitness routine, adhering to these five principles requires energy and vigilance. The results, however, will speak for themselves. Your sentences will become sturdier and more energetic, and your ideas will fit more comfortably on your newly shapely prose.

## Who needs the Writer's Diet?

Whether you are a student, an academic, a journalist, a fiction writer or even a poet, this book will help you develop healthy writing habits and see your own words with new eyes. Each chapter takes you on a guided tour of some of the world's finest sentences – and some truly dreadful ones as well. Along the way, you will learn how to pep up your prose without losing your sense of style.

Crucially, *The Writer's Diet* does not target beginning writers only. All too often, the most intellectually sophisticated authors are the ones who produce the most ungainly prose. Those who go on to pursue advanced academic degrees quickly learn the power of jargon, which functions within many professional spheres like a secret handshake among initiates. Over time, even the most experienced authors may lose their sense of perspective and come to regard impenetrable prose as "normal." This book furnishes a reality check, a way for you to measure your own writing against the best and worst by your colleagues.

*The Writer's Diet* provides no "big picture" advice on argument or audience, no instruction on composition or paragraph structure, no primer on "correct" grammar and punctuation. Instead, the book zeroes in on five common problems that frequently plague unfit sentences and offers practical exercises to help you develop healthier writing habits.

## The WritersDiet Test

The five chapters of this book correspond to the five sections of the WritersDiet Test, a tongue-in-cheek diagnostic instrument that tells you whether your writing is "flabby or fit." You can take the test online at www.writersdiet.com or follow the manual instructions at the back of the book.

Some writers use the WritersDiet Test to pinpoint problems in specific passages; others submit longer samples and try to identify overall patterns in their work. Either way, the test offers a heuristic, not a rigid formula or set of rules. Ask yourself: Did I write this way on purpose? Do I like the results?

The WritersDiet Test will help you identify signature patterns in your work: a weakness for *be*-verbs, perhaps, or a penchant for prepositional phrases. Maybe you will even spot some verbal tics not highlighted by the test itself. Many writers find that their scores change significantly depending on what kind of sample they test: a personal essay, for example, typically contains more concrete nouns and active verbs than an academic journal abstract, which is likely to be, well, more abstract.

"Can good writing really be reduced to a numerical formula?" you ask. No, of course not; the work of the world's finest authors will always resist quantitative analysis. The WritersDiet Test makes no attempt to measure for vividness of expression, clarity of thought, fluidity of style or any of the other elements that matter most in good writing. Confident stylists understand the value of flouting the rules, stretching the boundaries and even indulging from time to time in strategic excess.

## How to use this book

You can benefit from this book without taking the WritersDiet Test, and you can take the test without reading the book. However, the book and the test have been designed to work together as complementary tools. The test provides an immediate, personalized diagnosis, helping you identify some of the grammatical features that most frequently weigh down intelligent prose. The book explains those features in depth, lingering on stylistic subtleties and exceptions that the test cannot address. The test is a blunt instrument; the book coaches you in the complex human art of writing powerful prose.

If your writing feels stodgy and anemic but you have never quite been able to say why, the WritersDiet Test will *show* you in a visual, visceral way. The book, in turn, will help you interpret your test scores, figure out how to improve them and even decide when to ignore them. Many fabulous pieces of writing will come out looking "flabby" or worse on the WritersDiet Test, because stylish writers have the confidence and skill to play around with language in ways that the test is neither designed nor intended to evaluate. Examples at the end of each chapter will show you how to make sense of complex and even contradictory results.

Over time, as the core principles outlined in this book become habits of mind, you will probably discover that you no longer need the WritersDiet Test at all. Instead of writing bulky sentences and afterwards paring them down to size, you will find yourself producing taut, energetic prose every time you put pen to paper or fingers to keyboard.

# 1.

# Verbal verve

**Key principles in this chapter:**

- Favor strong, specific, robust action verbs (*scrutinize, dissect, recount, capture*) over weak, vague, lazy ones (*have, do, show*).
- Limit your use of *be*-verbs (*is, am, are, was, were, be, being, been*)

Verbs power our sentences as surely as muscles propel our bodies. In fact, a sentence is not technically a sentence unless it contains a verb. Not all verbs pack the same punch, however. Active verbs such as *grow, fling* and *exhale* infuse your writing with vigor and metaphorical zing; they put legs on your prose. Forms of the verbs *to be* – for example *is, was, are* – do their duty too, but they carry you nowhere new. Think of them as the gluteus maximus of your grammatical anatomy.

It is much easier to write a sentence that is dominated by *be*-verbs and passive constructions – such as the one you are reading right now – than to summon the energy to construct action-driven prose. After all, why waste time ferreting through your brain in search of varied, vivid verbs if that good old standby *is* will serve your sentences just as well?

Active verbs merit effort and attention for at least three reasons. First, they supply a sense of agency and urgency to your writing by telling you who did what to whom. A scientist's passive locution, "The research was performed," lacks the honesty and directness of "We performed the research."

Second, active verbs add force and complexity to otherwise static sentences. When you write, "The pandemic swept through South America," you implicitly liken the pandemic's effect to that of a fire sweeping through a forest or a broom sweeping clear a cluttered floor. "The pandemic was very serious" simply doesn't spark our imagination in the same way.

Third, active verbs demand economy and precision, whereas *be*-verbs invite sloppy syntax. Consider this flaccid sentence by a philosophy student:

> What is interesting about viruses is that their genetic stock is very meager.

A light workout – including the addition of a stronger verb and a fresh adverb – renders the sentence at once stronger and livelier:

> Viruses originate from a surprisingly meager genetic stock.

In sum, *be*-verbs function much like equal signs in a mathematical equation; rather than shifting a sentence into new territory, they describe the status quo. In a passive verb construction, a *be*-verb neutralizes an active verb like a spider trapping a honeybee: "He *was startled* by the bell"; "Her face *was lined* with wrinkles." Note how, in these sentences, the action words lose their status as verbs and take on the role of descriptive adjectives (*startled*, *lined*) instead.

When used in moderation, there's nothing wrong with *be*-verbs. We need *is* in our sentences just as we need starch in our diet and socks in our wardrobe. Forms of *be* can help us create subtle distinctions of agency, action and tense; for example, "I was made to feel inferior" means something quite different from "She made me feel inferior" or "I felt inferior." Likewise, "He is going shopping" suggests a different temporality than "He goes shopping" or "He shops every day."

*Be*-verbs become problematic only when we grow lazy: when *is* and *are* become the main staples of every sentence simply because we cannot be bothered to vary our verbs. The following excerpt from an undergraduate essay on cinematography offers a case in point:

> *American Beauty* is one of the best films I have ever seen.
> The Academy gave the movie a "Picture of the Year" award, among
> other honors. There are many good uses of cinematography
> throughout the film. I will be describing how cinematography is
> used to enhance what is happening in that particular scene.

*Be*-verbs (*is, are, be*) make up nearly 10% of the words in this passage. Two potentially active verbs, *describe* and *happen*, suffer from the weakening addition of *-ing*, which necessitates an accompanying form of *be* ("will *be* describing," "what *is* happening"). Meanwhile, the only remaining active verbs – *see, give, use, enhance* – prove so bland and generic that they contribute little more energy than *is* and *are*. When we strip away the *be*-verbs from the final sentence – "I will *be* describing how cinematography *is* used to enhance what *is* happening in that particular scene" – we reveal the core sentence that lurks beneath:

I will describe how cinematography enhances what happens in a
particular scene.

This new version retains the meaning of the original, but the word count
drops from 17 words to just 12 – a "lard factor" (to borrow a phrase from
Richard A. Lanham) of 29%.[1]

Accomplished authors do not ban *be*-verbs altogether. Instead, they
employ them carefully and in moderation, with occasional bursts of
strategic excess. For example, the opening sentence of Charles Dickens"
*A Tale of Two Cities* contains the *be*-verb *was* a whopping ten times:

> It was the best of times, it was the worst of times, it was the age of
> wisdom, it was the age of foolishness, it was the epoch of belief, it was
> the epoch of incredulity, it was the season of Light, it was the season
> of Darkness, it was the spring of hope, it was the winter of despair . . .[2]

Yet if you look at the pages that follow this *be*-verb bonanza, you
will find that they shimmer with active verbs. Having lulled us into
a sense of stasis and sameness with all those abstract *was*-phrases,
Dickens suddenly veers off into a colorful, verb-driven description of
pre-Revolutionary France:

> France, less favored on the whole as to matters spiritual than her sister
> of the shield and trident, rolled with exceeding smoothness down
> hill, making paper money and spending it. Under the guidance of her
> Christian pastors, she entertained herself, besides, with such humane
> achievements as sentencing a youth to have his hands cut off, his
> tongue torn out with pincers, and his body burned alive, because he
> had not kneeled down in the rain to do honour to a dirty procession
> of monks which passed within his view, at a distance of some fifty or
> sixty yards.

Rather than telling us directly that the political situation in France was grim, Dickens shows us a misguided nation that "*rolled* with exceeding smoothness down hill," like a severed head into a basket. Personifying France as a frivolous woman who "*entertained* herself" by staging events such as the youth's gruesome death – "his hands *cut* off, his tongue *torn* out with pincers, and his body *burned* alive, because he had not *kneeled* down in the rain" – Dickens draws an unspoken parallel to Marie Antoinette, the queen whose luxurious excesses would eventually inspire France's oppressed underclasses to revolt. In both cases, he relies not on overt comparisons – "France *was* like this or that" – but on active verbs that perform a much more subtle yet dramatic metaphorical function.

The most famous speech in Shakespeare's *Hamlet*, likewise, kicks off with three *be*-verbs in a row:

> To be, or not to be: that is the question.[3]

Faced with the stark choice between life or death, the tormented Prince Hamlet asks himself:

> Whether 'tis nobler in the mind to suffer
> The slings and arrows of outrageous fortune,
> Or to take arms against a sea of troubles,
> And by opposing end them?

The active verbs that animate this sentence – *suffer*, *take arms*, *oppose* – charge the prince's existential musings with a vivid physicality sustained through the rest of the soliloquy:

> Who would fardels bear,
> To grunt and sweat under a weary life,

But that the dread of something after death,
The undiscover'd country from whose bourn
No traveler returns, puzzles the will
And makes us rather bear those ills we have
Than fly to others that we know not of?

In Hamlet's grim vision of human existence, we must choose between two equally unsavory choices: to "grunt and sweat" and "bear those ills we have," or to leave our physical selves behind and fly to the "undiscover'd country" of death, from which "no traveler returns." Through his use of active verbs, Shakespeare portrays life (*to be*) as a painful burden and death (*not to be*) as a frightening journey.

Active verbs fire our imagination by appealing directly to the human senses; they invite us to see, hear, touch, taste and smell objects and ideas, rather than merely letting them *be*. Craft-conscious writers do not necessarily reach for a thesaurus every time they compose a new sentence. However, they do routinely exercise and stretch their vocabulary, seeking out verbs that convey visual imagery and action.

Observe, for example, the elegance and exactness of the verbs selected by Pulitzer-Prize-winning author John McPhee to describe how shad (a kind of fish) strike at a fisherman's lure:

> Flutter something colorful in their faces and shad will either ignore it completely or snap at it like pit bulls. More precisely, they'll swing their heads, as swordfish do, to bat an irritant aside. They don't swallow, since they're not eating. Essentially never does a hook reach the gills, or even much inside the mouth. You hook them in the mouth's outer rim – in the premaxillary and maxillary bones and sometimes in the ethmoid region at the tip of the snout, all of which are segments of the large open scoop that plows through plankton at sea.[4]

*Flutter, snap, swing, bat, swallow*: every one of these words expresses motion and activity. Note, too, how McPhee paces his verbs. In the first four sentences of the passage, he hurls them at us thick and fast, fluttering action words in our faces like brightly colored lures. In the fifth sentence, however, McPhee withholds his final verb, offering a long string of prepositional phrases – "*in* the premaxillary and maxillary bones and sometimes *in* the ethmoid region *at* the tip *of* the snout" – before hooking his readers at last with his striking description of the shad's mouth as a "large open scoop that *plows* through plankton at sea."

Contrast McPhee's verb-driven sentences with the following examples from peer-reviewed scientific journal articles in computer science and evolutionary biology, respectively:

> [Computer science] A schema mapping is a specification that describes how data structured under one schema (the source schema) is to be transformed into data structured under a different schema (the target schema). Although the notion of an inverse of a schema mapping is important, the exact definition of an inverse mapping is somewhat elusive.[5]

> [Evolutionary biology] Species complexes are composed of genetically isolated lineages that are not distinguishable on the basis of purely morphological criteria. Such difficulties have been encountered in almost all taxonomic groups, even the most studied birds and mammals. . . . Detecting the cryptic structure of species complexes is essential for an accurate accounting of the biological diversity in natural systems.[6]

*Is, describes, is to be; are, have been, is.* Many academics mistakenly believe that such bland, agentless prose expresses scientific ideas more accurately and objectively than the metaphorically rich language of fiction writers and poets. But good writing need not imply bad science:

> [Computer science] Either we can scan, or "crawl," the text database or, alternatively, we can exploit search engine indexes and retrieve the documents of interest via carefully crafted queries constructed in task-specific ways. . . . Reputation management systems download Web pages to track the "buzz" around companies and products. Comparative shopping agents locate e-commerce Web sites and add the products offered in the pages to their own index.[7]

> [Evolutionary biology] Insects suck, chew, parasitize, bore, store, and even cultivate their foods to a highly sophisticated degree of specialization, and much of the evolution of the group appears to be related to the way in which insects interact with their environment by feeding.[8]

In these extracts from journal articles in the same two disciplines as the previous examples, active verbs do much more than merely supply local color to otherwise beige prose. Carefully selected verbs such as *scan, crawl, exploit, retrieve, download, track, locate, suck, chew, parasitize, bore, store, cultivate* and *interact* communicate their authors' meaning with scientific rigor and precision.

In the following excerpt from an undergraduate essay on abortion, note how the energy of the opening question dissipates in the second sentence, which is choked with *be*-verbs:

> Pro-Life or Pro-Choice? That is a big question that a lot of Catholics are asked.

With minimal exertion, we can eliminate the two *be* phrases (*that is, are asked*) and pump up the power of the verb:

Pro-Life or Pro-Choice? Many Catholics grapple with this difficult question.

Not only have we cut the word count of the second sentence from 12 to 7 – a lard factor of 41% – but our new, improved sentence conveys a sense of mental deliberation and moral struggle absent from the original. The verb *grapple* supplies a physical metaphor for the otherwise abstract mental process of choosing between two moral positions. And the Catholics have now become the subjects rather than the objects of the sentence, the agents rather than the recipients of the action. We picture them actively engaging with the pro-life/pro-choice question, rather than politely "being asked" to think about it.

Running up a steep incline requires more effort than standing still or walking slowly along a flat surface. Likewise, writing lively sentences requires more effort than relying on forms of *be* and other bland, abstract verbs. Indeed, one could argue that the laws of physics apply (metaphorically, at least) to grammar as well as to objects. *Is* equals inertia; and we know from Newton's First Law that a body at rest will remain at rest until acted upon by an external force. By the same token, a stodgy sentence will remain inert until its author exerts the force to rouse it.

# Exercises

The following exercises will stretch and tone your verbal muscles. Feel free to concoct your own variations.

## *From passive to active*

Identify five sentences that employ the passive voice – either in your own writing or in someone else's work – and turn them into active sentences that contain no forms of *be*. In doing so, you might have to furnish new verbs or even rephrase entire sentences.

    **Example:** The passengers **were asked** to return to their seats.

Who asked the passengers to return to their seats? To render this sentence active, we need to identify the agent who performs the action. Try out some different possibilities and attend to their nuances:

- The flight attendant **asked** the passengers to return to their seats.
- The captain **told** the passengers to return to their seats.
- The voice on the loudspeaker **ordered** the passengers to return to their seats.

Nearly all good writers employ the passive voice occasionally: for instance, to emphasize the initial noun in a sentence ("His face had been scarred by the experiences of a lifetime"), to avoid an intrusive "I" ("The book and the test have been designed to work together") or to enact a character's powerlessness ("his hands cut off, his tongue torn out with pincers, his body burned alive"). But sometimes the mere exercise of shifting to the active voice can lead to unexpected insights. For example, "The students *were taught*" takes on quite a different meaning when you write instead, "The teacher *instructed* the students" or "The students *learned*."

## From lazy to lively

Select a short sample of your writing – a paragraph or a page – and identify all the verbs. Once you have eliminated the forms of *be*, what verbs remain? Many so-called "active" verbs – words like *make, do* and *use* – convey no specific sense of action. Can you liven up your prose by replacing bland, predictable verbs with more precise, energetic alternatives?

> **Example:** Many people in Russia **have** no skills in Internet usage. Those people **include** the young as well as the older generations.

By the time we have finished reading these opening lines from an undergraduate essay on Internet use in Russia, we are already nodding off. Rather than merely replacing *have* with *possess* – the lazy option, rather like substituting *utilize* for *use* – let's try *lack*, a verb that emphasizes absence and deficiency. Next, we can fold the two sentences together:

> Many people in Russia – the young as well as the older generations – **lack** Internet skills.

Why do the Russians lack Internet skills? Will this situation lead to adverse social and educational consequences? The new opening sentence makes us want to keep reading to find out the answers to these questions.

## Energy bars for the brain

Set a timer for five minutes and write down all the active verbs you can think of. Allow your mind to wander, romp and play. Keep your list of interesting verbs on hand whenever you sit down to write, and add to it as new ones occur to you. Like energy bars for an athlete, your stash of "verbs with verve" will supply needed fuel when your verbal energy begins to flag.

### WritersDiet Test example 1

In this article I am going to distinguish different levels of social practice and psychic subjectification within which it is possible to describe shifts in the regulation of gender. The more abstract level of my argument is that it is helpful to maintain a distinction between changes in the codes regulating practices within social fields, and changes at the level of gender as a primary mark of human subjectivity within the Symbolic Order. At a more concrete level, I am arguing that, while it is possible to identify gendered shifts in the codification of disciplinary and pedagogic practices within universities, the subjectivity of individual academics is still primarily embodied within the codes of hegemonic heterosexual gender identities.[9]

---

**WritersDiet fitness ratings:**

| | |
|---|---|
| verbs | Heart attack |
| nouns | Heart attack |
| prepositions | Heart attack |
| adjectives/adverbs | Heart attack |
| it, this, that, there | Flabby |
| **Overall** | **Heart attack** |

---

**Comments:** *Be*-verbs, abstract nouns and academic adjectives dominate this unwieldy passage from a peer-reviewed higher education journal. Abstract verbs such as *distinguish, describe, maintain, argue* and *identify* fail to perk things up much. The third sentence promisingly begins, "At a more concrete level. . . ." However, no concrete images or examples reveal themselves here.

# 2.

# Noun density

**Key principles in this chapter:**
- Anchor abstract ideas in concrete language and images.
- Illustrate abstract concepts using real-life examples. ("Show, don't tell.")
- Limit your use of abstract nouns, especially nominalizations (nouns that have been formed from verbs, adjectives or other nouns).

If verbs function as the muscles of language, nouns form its bones. Sentences with "strong bones" convey meaning and emotion through concrete nouns, which describe objects we can see, hear, touch, taste or smell, such as *water*, *hands* or *moon*. Sentences with "weak bones" rely mostly on abstract nouns, which express intangible ideas remote from the world of the human senses. We can talk and think and argue about *sadness* and *affection* and *reciprocity*, but these concepts bear no physical weight.

Compare the following two accounts of the imaginative development of children, the first by poet Robert Morgan, the second by a team of psychology researchers:

> **Poet:**     More than
> all I loved to slide the hatpins
> like adjustable rods in the
> plum-shaped cushion . . . I
> knew without asking I wouldn't be
> allowed such deadly probes and heart-
> picks. Some were long as witches' wands
> with fat pearl heads. They slid in the
> cushion as through waxy flesh.
> I extracted a cold silver
> excalibur and ran it on
> my wrist and stabbed at the mirror,
> then froze, listening for her step.[10]

> **Psychologists:** As children develop the ability to transition between states, they can be thought of as becoming less dissociative. In this way, non-pathological dissociation may be connected to Theory of Mind, inhibitory control and other metacognitive abilities of interest to developmental researchers. Another line of research has connected non-pathological dissociation to fantasy proneness or imagination.[11]

The poem illustrates how a grandmother's hatpins become, in the eyes of a child, witches' wands and magicians' swords. Concrete nouns and vivid verbs – *rods, cushion, probes, heartpicks, heads, flesh, excalibur, wrist, mirror; slid, extracted, ran, stabbed, froze* – provide a window into the child's mixed emotions of desire, fascination and fear. The academic article, by contrast, swathes children and researchers in a cloud

of abstractions: *ability, state, dissociation, theory, mind, control, interest.*
The authors offer us no descriptive signposts to guide our understanding, no heartpicks or excaliburs on which to hang an emotional or
intellectual response.

And now here is a passage by Alison Gopnik, a psychologist who
writes with a poet's flair:

> [A researcher] asked randomly chosen three- and four-year-old
> children and their parents a set of specific questions about imaginary
> companions. Most of the children, 63 percent to be exact, described
> a vivid, often somewhat bizarre, imaginary creature. . . . Many of
> the imaginary companions had a poetic appeal: Baintor, who was
> invisible because he lived in the light; Station Pheta, who hunted
> sea anemones on the beach. Sometimes the companions were other
> children but sometimes they were dwarves or dinosaurs. Sometimes
> the children became the imaginary creatures themselves.[12]

Concrete nouns – *children, parents, creatures, companions; light, sea
anemones, dwarves, dinosaurs* – do double duty in this paragraph. First,
they illustrate Gopnik's central argument that children are "young scientists" with a highly developed capacity for counterfactual thinking.
Second, Gopnik has chosen examples calculated to engage and charm
her readers. An abstract concept such as "non-pathological disassoci-
ation" becomes much more memorable and inviting when it takes the
form of an invisible friend called Baintor.

All too often, academics swarm to abstract language like pigs to mud;
they wallow in big words and explain, explain, explain. Poets and fiction
writers, on the other hand, prefer to illustrate abstract ideas through
physical images and concrete examples: "Show, don't tell." For example, here's how poet Emily Dickinson depicts *hope*, that most fragile yet
resilient of human emotions:

Hope is the thing with feathers
That perches in the soul,
And sings the tune without the words
And never stops at all.[13]

Here's how novelist A. S. Byatt conveys a character's mixed feelings of nostalgia, passion and revulsion upon recalling a past love affair:

Her mind was full of an image of a huge, unmade, stained and rumpled bed, its sheets pulled into standing peaks here and there, like the surface of whipped egg-white. Whenever she thought of [her former lover], this empty battlefield was what she saw.[14]

And here's how popular science writer Dava Sobel illustrates the historical importance of longitude, that made-up measurement by which human beings define their place on the globe:

The zero-degree parallel of latitude is fixed by the laws of nature, while the zero-degree meridian of longitude shifts like the sands of time. This difference makes finding latitude child's play, and turns the determination of longitude, especially at sea, into an adult dilemma – one that stumped the wisest minds of the world for the better part of human history. . . . For lack of a practical method of determining longitude, every great captain in the Age of Exploration became lost at sea despite the best available charts and compasses.[15]

These authors show us that concrete language is the ally of abstract thought, not its enemy. Sobel's descriptive passage contains more than a dozen abstract nouns: *longitude, latitude, parallel, law, nature, meridian, time, difference, play, determination, dilemma, mind, history, method.* However, the author grounds these intangible concepts in the physical world with active verbs (*shift, find, turn, stump*), tactile metaphors (*sands of time, child's play*) and illustrative examples ("every great captain in the Age of Exploration became lost at sea despite the best available charts and compasses"). Through her strategic use of concrete language, Sobel persuades her readers to care about the historical impact of an imaginary line. Picture the same subject matter in the hands of a less skillful author:

> Latitude is a naturally occurring measurement that can be
> determined by a simple calculation of equatorial displacement.
> Longitude, by contrast, is a man-made construct that depends on the
> arbitrary designation of a prime meridian and therefore cannot be
> measured using conventional astronomical instruments alone.

Clear? Yes. Compelling? Not particularly.

Even when she does employ abstract language, note how Sobel favors punchy, varied nouns such as *law, nature, mind, history* and *time* over spongy, sing-songy ones such as *measurement, calculation, displacement* and *designation*. When you turn a verb into a noun by adding a suffix such as *ment* or *tion* (*confine → confinement; reflect → reflection*), you sap its core energy. Likewise, an abstract noun formed from an adjective (*suspicious → suspiciousness*) or a concrete noun (*globe → globalization*) tends to lack substance and mass, like a marrowless bone. That's why nouns created from other parts of speech, technically known as "nominalizations," are colloquially called "zombie nouns": they suck the lifeblood from potentially lively prose.[16]

Banishing zombie nouns – or even reducing their numbers – may require you to rethink your subject matter as well as your writing style. In extreme cases, you might even have to rewrite entire passages from scratch. The following excerpt from an academic article on business management is bloated with nominalizations:

The capacity of a decision unit to induce innovation implementation within an adoption unit is crucial to organizational success.
Risk and complexity are characteristics of innovations that can lead
to resistance within organizational adoption units. Communication
costs, types of power, and communication channels are structural
characteristics that can be used by a decision unit to overcome
this resistance. The interaction of these factors can determine
the degree of successful innovation implementation within
organizations.[17]

What are the authors really trying to say here? The highly abstract title
of the article, "Communication and Innovation Implementation," does
not help us out much. Nor do the abstract nouns and compound noun
phrases (*capacity, success, risk, complexity, characteristics, innovations,
resistance, types, power, interaction, factors, degree, organizations, decision unit, innovation implementation, adoption unit, communication
costs, communication channels*), the noun-derived adjectives (*crucial,
organizational, structural*), the leaden verbs (*induce, lead, determine*) or
the multiple forms of *be* (*is, are, are*). This passage requires the editorial
equivalent of gastric band surgery.

Once we have discarded most of the jargon, transformed *decision
units* and *adoption units* into human beings, and located the paragraph's
center of gravity, we end up with a small, hard core of meaning:

Organizations thrive on change; however, many employees resist new
ideas that they perceive as too risky or complex. Successful managers
break down such resistance by communicating with staff clearly and
strategically.

Now the passage describes real people making real decisions about
how to run a company, rather than automatons involved in "innovation

implementation." Concrete nouns (*employees, managers*) and active verbs (*resist, perceive, communicate, break down*) provide ballast for a few key abstractions (*ideas, organization, resistance*). Having trimmed the word count from 73 to 31 (a lard factor of 58%), we have freed up space for an example illustrating *how* structural features such as "communication costs, types of power, and communication channels" can help bring about change within an organization.

Examples, analogies and metaphors ground abstract theories in the physical world; in Shakespeare's memorable phrasing, they give "to airy nothing / A local habitation and a name."[18] For example, "Big Bang" theorist George Smoot deploys the image of a dust mote on an ice rink to describe the challenges faced by cosmologists investigating the background radiation of the universe:

> We were looking for tiny variations in the smooth background temperatures, something less than one part in a hundred thousand – that is something like trying to spot a dust mote lying on a vast, smooth surface like a skating rink. And, just like a skating rink, there would be many irregularities on the surface that had nothing to do with those we sought.[19]

Philosopher Kwame Anthony Appiah illuminates the universality of the human condition by inventing a time-traveling baby:

> Our ancestors have been human for a very long time. If a normal baby girl born forty thousand years ago were kidnapped by a time traveler and raised in a normal family in New York, she would be ready for college in eighteen years. She would learn English (along with – who knows? – Spanish or Chinese), understand trigonometry, follow baseball and pop music; she would probably want a pierced tongue and a couple of tattoos.[20]

Essayist Joan Didion draws on images of back alleys, sleeping pills and uncomfortable beds to illustrate the corrosive effects of self-deception:

> The tricks that work on others count for nothing in that very well-lit back alley where one keeps assignations with oneself: no winning smiles will do here, no prettily drawn list of good intentions. . . . To live without self-respect is to lie awake some night, beyond the reach of warm milk, Phenobarbital, and the sleeping hand on the coverlet. . . . However long we postpone it, we eventually lie down alone in that notoriously uncomfortable bed, the one we make ourselves.[21]

If, after reading this chapter, you still doubt the emotional impact of concrete language, try sitting through a typical high school graduation address ("We encourage our students to achieve their highest potentiality by continually striving for excellence," blah blah blah . . .), then go home and listen to a recording of Martin Luther King Jr's "I Have a Dream" speech, delivered from the steps of the Lincoln Memorial in Washington, D.C. on a hot August day in 1963. Through the first half of his speech, King read aloud from a prepared text drafted by a committee. But then he arrived at the following sentence, teeming with nominalizations:

> And so today, let us go back to our communities as members of the international association for the advancement of creative dissatisfaction.[22]

At that point King laid his written text – and his abstract language – aside:

> I have a dream that one day on the red hills of Georgia, the sons of former slaves and the sons of former slave owners will be able to sit

down at the table of brotherhood. I have a dream that one day even the state of Mississippi, a state sweltering with the heat of injustice, sweltering with the heat of oppression, will be transformed into an oasis of freedom and justice. I have a dream that my four little children will one day live in a nation where they will not be judged by the color of their skin but by the content of their character.

In King's vision of a post-racial America, intangible concepts such as *brotherhood, oppression, freedom, justice* and *character* take on a physical presence and a human form: *red hills, table, heat, oasis, my four little children, the color of their skin.* And that is why, unlike the worthy platitudes of the typical high school principal or politician, King's words still echo in our minds and hearts today.

# Exercises

These exercises will sharpen your sensibility for concrete language and build up the noun density of your prose.

## *Grammatical forensics*

Make a list of abstract nouns that carry the nominalizing suffixes *ion*, *ism*, *ty*, *ment*, *ness*, *ance* or *ence*. Next, identify the grammatical root stock on which each of these nouns grows. In most cases, you will find that the noun stems from a verb, an adjective or both.

**Examples:**
- **participation** (noun) → **participate** (verb)
- **conservatism** (noun) → **conservative** (adjective) → **conserve** (verb)
- **activity** (noun) → **active** (adjective) → **act** (verb/noun)
- **engagement** (noun) → **engage** (verb)
- **surveillance** (noun) → **survey** (verb)
- **excellence** (noun) → **excellent** (adjective) → **excel** (verb)

Now write a sentence that contains two or more of the abstract nouns on your list.

**Example:** The children demonstrated their **engagement** through their **participation** in a range of **activities**.

Experiment with ways of communicating the same information more concretely, whether by converting some of the nouns to verbs or adjectives or by replacing abstract language with concrete examples:

- The children engaged in many different activities.
- The children played games, sang songs and told stories.

### *Abstract to concrete and back again*

On a blank sheet of paper, write an abstract noun and draw an oval around it, adding six or more radiating spokes. At the end of each spoke, write a concrete image that exemplifies the abstract noun in the centre.

**Example:**

```
                    stacks of manila folders
                              |
      men in grey suits       |        red tape
                    \         |        /
                      (  BUREAUCRACY  )
                    /         |        \
      rubber stamps           |        filing cabinets
                              |
                    lines of grumpy-looking people
```

Now repeat the exercise, placing a concrete noun in the center and abstract nouns at the spoke ends.

**Example:**

```
                        warmth
                          |
      destruction         |         anger
              \           |           /
                \       ( FIRE )      /
              /           |           \
      passion             |         purification
                          |
                    enlightenment
```

Just about any idea or emotion can be illustrated using concrete images. Likewise, a single concrete noun can invoke a surprisingly complex range of abstractions. Good writers exploit the relationship between concrete and abstract language by remaining attentive to the subtleties of both.

# WritersDiet Test example 2

How are names for new disciplinary fields coined? Here a new (and fun) way to look at the history of such coinages is proposed, focusing on how phonesthemic tints and taints figure in decisions to adopt one type of suffix rather than another. The most common suffixes used in such coinages ("-logy," "-ics," etc.) convey semantic and evaluative content quite unpredictable from literal (root) meanings alone. Pharmaceutical manufacturers have long grasped the point, but historians have paid little attention to how suffixes of one sort or another become productive. A romp through examples from English shows that certain suffixes have become "hard" or "soft" in consequence of the status of their most prominent carrier disciplines.[23]

**WritersDiet fitness ratings:**

| | |
|---|---|
| verbs | Lean |
| nouns | Lean |
| prepositions | Needs toning |
| adjectives / adverbs | Needs toning |
| it, this, that, there | Lean |
| **Overall** | **Fit & trim** |

**Comments:** In this exuberant abstract for a journal article, historian Robert Proctor intersperses "zombie nouns" such as *decisions*, *attention* and *consequence* with unusual nouns such as *tint*, *taint* and *romp*. Active verbs (*look, figure, grasp*) contribute further energy and elan, while indigestible academic adjectives such as *disciplinary*, *phonesthemic*, *semantic* and *evaluative* become more palatable when washed down with easy-to-swallow words such as *new*, *"hard," "soft"* and even *fun*.[24]

# 3.

# Prepositional podge

**Key principles in this chapter:**
- Avoid using more than three prepositional phrases in a row (e.g. "*in* a letter *to* the author *of* a book *about* birds") unless you do so to achieve a specific rhetorical effect.
- Vary your prepositions.
- As a general rule, do not allow a noun and its accompanying verb to become separated by more than about twelve words.

Nouns and verbs form the building blocks of our sentences; but where would we be without prepositions? If we had none of those little linking words like *in* or *on* to help us position ourselves in the world, we would lose our sense of place. Try writing a preposition-free sentence, like the one you are reading right now, and you will feel handcuffed, shackled, frustrated. Why? Because prepositions expand the horizons of our sentences; they lasso new nouns and supply our verbs with directional thrust.

Too many prepositions, however, can slow a sentence down. Richard A. Lanham, author of a book called *Editing Prose*, observes that:

> Two prepositional phrases in a row turn on a warning light, three make a problem, and four invite disaster. . . . The *of* strings are the worst of all. They seem to reenact a series of hiccups.[25]

No wonder a phrase like

> an abandonment *of* the contemporary vision *of* a community *of* practice grounded *in* the experience *of* teachers

leaves us feeling dazed and confused.

Have you ever read a sentence that consists of lots of little phrases arranged in a series of grammatical units in which the main ideas have been constructed from an assortment of prepositions paired with lots of different kinds of nouns? Or perhaps at some point you have lost your way in a meandering sentence that seemed to drag on and on, wending its way past one topic after another, toiling up high rhetorical slopes, plunging down into valleys of introspection, urging you along through a series of insights until at last you staggered over the finish line and out of the prepositional mire? If so, you know the overwhelming, sometimes stultifying effect of too many prepositions.

Let's look more closely at the two long sentences in the preceding paragraph. In the first one, bland prepositions smother an already bland sentence, like a white sauce poured over baked cauliflower:

> Have you ever read a paragraph that consists of lots of little phrases arranged in a series of grammatical units in which the main ideas have been constructed from an assortment of prepositions paired with lots of different kinds of nouns?

When static prepositions that take you nowhere new (*of, in, from, with*) link together bundles of abstract nouns (*paragraph, phrases, series, units, assortment, prepositions, range, kinds, nouns*), we end up with a lengthy, diffuse sentence that in fact has very little to say. Similar constructions abound in academic prose:

> The use of cybernetics for this purpose is not obvious, because cybernetics – a science first developed in the 40s and 50s in the U.S. by Norbert Wiener and John von Neumann – implied to many critics in the socialist world an abandonment of the Marxist vision of a practice based in the experience of class struggle in favor of "system-neutral," "value-free" technocratic reason.[26]

Five repeated prepositions (*of, for, in, by, to*) allow the author of this sentence to cram in multiple abstract nouns (*use, cybernetics, purpose, science, abandonment, vision, practice, experience, struggle, reason*). Rather than helping us navigate, the excessive prepositions disorient us and bog us down.

Our second sample sentence, by contrast, shows how dynamic directional prepositions can propel a reader forward:

> Or perhaps at some point you have lost your way in a sentence that seemed to drag on and on, wending its way past one topic after another, toiling up high rhetorical slopes, plunging down into valleys of introspection, urging you along through a series of insights until at last you staggered across the finish line and out of the prepositional mire?

With its cliché-studded spatial metaphor and over-the-top rhetoric, this sentence arguably bears us beyond the pale of good writing and into the realm of purple prose. Yet it does so with good humor, poking fun at meandering, mazy sentences just like itself. Note how the varied prepositions (*at, in, on, past, after, up, down, into, of, along, through, until, across, out*) collaborate with nouns, verbs and other parts of speech to supply the sentence's energy: colorful -*ing* verbs (*wending, toiling, plunging, urging*) and other action verbs (*lost, drag, staggered*) anchor abstract ideas (*topic, introspection, effort*) in concrete imagery (*slopes, valleys, eyes, brain, finish line, mire*). We end up with a vivid mental image of a heroic reader conquering a marathon-length sentence.

In the hands of a self-conscious stylist, prepositions can draw out a moment of narrative suspense, mimic the stages of a journey or reinforce a sense of place. When poet Michele Leggott threads multiple prepositions through her architectural tour of ancient Babylon, she does so with a deft awareness of their rhapsodic, highly spatialized effect:

> city of delights now I walk barefoot
> on the glazed bricks of Babylon
> through white daisies on high walls
> among rippling yellow lions
> in tanks of blue protective grace
> to the catastrophe of Light beyond
> the Ishtar Gate[27]

Elsewhere, when she wants to communicate a different kind of dislocation, Leggott uses no prepositions at all:

> signature pink, leap
> bodily the helix enough
> doubled erotic or singing to
> say I am energy make
> certain my best feints dab
> your ever, this is me[28]

These two examples show us how a confident writer's diet can change radically from one repast to the next: muesli and yogurt for breakfast, strawberries and champagne for lunch, fish and chips for dinner.

In academic writing, prepositions tend to become a problem only when authors jumble ideas and asides together a bit too enthusiastically, as in this example from a peer-reviewed literary studies journal:

> A number of artists, most of them with French connections, but with little else in common than their deep involvement in visual interpretations of literary masterpieces, have provided new settings for, and found new meanings in, Gertrude Stein's often hermetic texts.[29]

This serpentine sentence contains numerous prepositional phrases and other subordinate clauses, which in turn dilute the sentence's energy by placing an excessive distance between its main noun and its verbs. Indeed, seven prepositions – *of*, *of*, *with*, *with*, *in*, *in*, *of* – intervene between the subject ("a number") and the first accompanying verb ("have provided"). When stripped of its subordinate clauses, the passage reads much more clearly:

> A number of artists have provided new settings for, and found new meanings in, Gertrude Stein's often hermetic texts.

However, the revised version lacks the subtlety, detail and rhythmic flow of the original. The author probably needs to seek a middle ground between the two: a way of bringing the subject and verb closer together without abandoning breadth and nuance.

Some readers, especially those with a high level of intellectual stamina who have been trained in the consumption of syntactically complex academic prose, can stretch their attention span to accommodate, say, twenty or more words between subject and verb, as you have just managed to do with this sentence:

> Some **readers**, especially those with a high level of intellectual
> stamina who have been trained in the consumption of syntactically complex academic prose, **can stretch** their attention span to
> accommodate, say, twenty or more words between subject and verb.

Few mortals, however, can cope with the grammatical intricacies of a sentence like this one from the scholarly journal *Postmodern Culture*:

> The **possibility** that the "man," whose being seems so self-evident
> and whose nature provides the object of modern knowledge and
> the human sciences, will one day be erased as a figure in thought **is**
> precisely what Foucault's genealogy of the human sciences in *The
> Order of Things* sets out to entertain.[30]

No fewer than 31 words interpose between the sentence's highly abstract subject (*possibility*) and its main verb (*is*). A concrete subject and an active verb would help invigorate this puffy prose. An even more serious problem, however, lies in the distance between noun and verb. To avoid such strung-out syntax, many authors stick to the "dynamic dozen" rule: avoid separating subject and verb by more than about twelve words, unless you have a very good reason for doing so.

While experienced academics tend to pack on the prepositional pudge, less confident writers may suffer from preposition deprivation. Consider this passage by a high school history student:

> Many factors caused the United States to declare war upon Mexico.
> For example, the two nations spoke different languages and had
> different religions. The United States was full of energy and trying

to expand. Mexico had little unity, was sparsely populated, and was weakened due to an oppressive upper class. The American mind was thinking about Manifest Destiny, and Mexico had control over Texas, California, and New Mexico.

The prose is lucid, concise, devoid of flab – and rather dull. Each sentence contains a subject, a verb, an object, one or two prepositional phrases and little else. Descriptive action verbs would help perk things up, as would some illustrative examples, some well-placed adjectives and, yes, a few more prepositional phrases. As we see from this example, leanness of style does not necessarily guarantee elegance and eloquence. Indeed, excessively economical prose may signal verbal anorexia.

Prepositions add motion and direction to otherwise static language; they position our nouns (*a bug in the rug, a cat on the mat*) and shift the meaning of our verbs (*shut in, shut out, shut off, shut up*). Imagine these famous titles without their prepositions: *Back to the Future, From Russia with Love, On the Waterfront, Outside over There, Through the Looking-Glass, To the Lighthouse, Up the Down Staircase.*

When advised by a conservative editor that he should avoid ending any sentence with a preposition, Winston Churchill reportedly retorted, "That is the sort of nonsense up with which I will not put!" By mocking the editor's edict through the very act of obeying it, Churchill affirmed the power of prepositions. Whether or not we put up with them, we cannot easily put them aside.

# Exercises

The following exercises will help you combat prepositional pudge and strengthen links between nouns and verbs.

## *Prepositions with pep*

Choose a page or two of your own writing and highlight all the prepositions. Next, ask yourself the following questions:

- Do you ever use more than three or four prepositional phrases in a row? (e.g. "a book **of** case studies **about** the efficacy **of** involving multiple stakeholders **in** discussions **about** health care")
- Are your prepositions dynamic or static? That is, do they suggest action and motion (**through**, **onto**, **from**), or do they reinforce the status quo (**in**, **of**, **by**)?
- Do you vary your prepositions, or do you tend to use the same two or three over and over again?

Play around with ways of making your prose glide more smoothly. For example, what happens when you cut long strings of prepositions down to size, or when you replace static prepositions with dynamic ones, or when you ensure the word *of* occurs no more than two or three times in a single paragraph?

## *Commuter marriage*

Although nouns and verbs can communicate with each other across wide distances, they function most harmoniously at close range. Choose a paragraph or two of your writing and identify the subject of each sentence, along with its accompanying verb. Do you find any sentences in which the subject and verb are separated by more than about twelve words? If so, try rephrasing them so that noun and verb walk hand in hand.

> **Example:** The **nub** of the issue, which philosophers in earlier centuries tended to dismiss as irrelevant, but which recent thinkers have come to regard as the centerpiece of our awareness of ourselves as human beings, **depends** on whether or not we are willing to accept a world without God.

The subject of the above sentence, *nub*, and the verb, *depends*, call out to each other across 32 intervening words. When we reunite subject and verb by breaking the sentence into three shorter ones (and chopping out a few prepositional phrases along the way), we end up with trimmer, cleaner prose:

> The nub of the issue depends on our willingness to accept a world without God. In earlier centuries, philosophers tended to dismiss this issue as irrelevant. Recent thinkers, however, have come to regard it as the centerpiece of human self-awareness.

However, our revision exposes a crucial flaw in the original sentence: *nub* and *depend* do not in fact work well together. (Can a *nub depend* on something?) A meticulous author would rethink – and rewrite – the entire paragraph yet again.

# WritersDiet Test example 3

The switch from the axis of presence and absence to the axis of pattern and randomness helps to explain one of the oddest dynamics in this odd poem: the recurrent whisking of characters through switchpoints between contexts. Such transfers occur in a spark or a flash: the glance exchanged by Helen and Achilles at Troy, the blast as Helen vanishes down a set of spiral stairs during the fall of Troy, the flash in the heavens on the beach in Egypt. In each of these moments, we are asked to imagine the transmission of patterns from one context to another. [31]

**WritersDiet fitness ratings:**

| | |
|---|---|
| verbs | Lean |
| nouns | Fit & trim |
| prepositions | Heart attack |
| adjectives/adverbs | Lean |
| it, this, that, there | Lean |
| **Overall** | **Flabby** |

**Comments:** In this passage by literary critic Adalaide Morris, the multiple prepositions create a sense of displacement and link together concrete nouns – *switchpoints*, *spark*, *flash*, *glance*, *Helen*, *Achilles*, *Troy*, *blast*, *stairs*, *flash*, *heavens*, *beach*, *Egypt* – that embody the abstract themes of *presence*, *absence*, *randomness* and *pattern*. Because her prepositions serve a clear structural purpose, the author can safely ignore her "Heart attack" rating in this category and leave the paragraph unchanged.

# 4.

# Ad-dictions

**Key principles in this chapter:**
- Let concrete nouns and active verbs do most of your descriptive work.
- Employ adjectives and adverbs only when they contribute new information to a sentence.
- Avoid overuse of "academic *ad*-words," especially those with the following suffixes: *able, ac, al, ant, ary, ent, ful, ible, ic, ive, less, ous*

Primary school teachers often encourage their pupils to jazz up their writing with "sizzle words": that is, with lots of adjectives and adverbs. Thus a cat inevitably becomes "a *creeping* cat" or "a *mysterious* cat" or "a *fluffy* cat." No one would deny the impact of a well-placed adjective. However, a sentence crammed with too many artificial additives can function in your prose like a creamy sauce or a sugary cake in your diet: despite its seductive taste, it supplies no real nutrition.

*Ad*-words cannot stand on their own; an adjective always modifies a noun or a pronoun (a *beautiful* day; I was *happy*), while an adverb modifies either a verb (to play *gently*), an adjective (*painfully* shy) or another adverb (*blissfully* slowly). *Ad*-words lend color and flavor to our writing; they help us express emotions, describe appearances and define character. Sometimes, however, they sugar-coat weak sentences that lack active verbs and concrete nouns.

Novice writers often find themselves drawn to *ad*-words like magpies to rhinestones, mistakenly believing that adjectives will add sparkle and flair to their writing. For example, this undergraduate student's fictional account of a Hindu woman's life contains nearly as many *ad*-words as nouns:

> As Reva carefully opened the temple door, she noticed the bright light filter in from the hot afternoon sun. The slight woman placed a small, brightly colored package of food on the ground and began to pray to Shiva, the destroyer and regenerator. Underneath her ghungat, Reva felt the sweat trickle down her tanned neck and off her blackened brow. She felt faint, to think of her upcoming fate.

A few of these adjectives and adverbs, such as *slight* and *brightly colored*, contribute significant visual details to the story. Others merely add empty calories. Does the author really need to tell us that the light is *bright* and the sun is *hot*? Or that Reva's neck is *tanned* and her brow *blackened*? The power of this passage radiates from its active verbs and concrete nouns, which show rather than tell us how to feel. A woman eases open the door of a temple; she places an offering of food on the ground and prays to a holy statue; sweat trickles down her neck. The surfeit of *ad*-words (*carefully, bright, hot, small, tanned, blackened*) detracts from, rather than contributes to, the impact of the passage.

Skillful writers can set a scene, paint a character or convey emotions using remarkably few adjectives. Here's how novelist Glen David Gold describes a phantasmagoric performance by an early-twentieth-century magician:

> Carter moved to the back of the house when Mysterioso's end-of-the-bill program began. After much to-do by stilt-walkers and fire-eaters, a trio of bloodthirsty Indians rushed from the wings with hatchets. Just as the performers looked as if they would be scalped, Mysterioso appeared on horseback, waving the American flag and shouting. He swung his cavalry saber, beheading one man and, using a rope that seemed to defy gravity, stringing another up from the rafters. The third Indian managed to manacle Mysterioso and escape with a beautiful woman. A volunteer was called onstage to check the handcuffs and see if it were possible for the magician to escape from them. But regardless of how the volunteer tugged and twisted, the network of handcuffs and chains was seemingly impossible to escape. Seconds later, however, the magician managed to shrug off the bonds, mount his horse, and swear revenge.[32]

Aside from *bloodthirsty, beautiful, impossible* and *possible*, this action-packed passage from Gold's novel *Carter Beats the Devil* contains virtually no *ad*-words. Instead, vibrant verbs (*rush, scalp, swing, behead, manacle, escape, tug, twist, shrug, mount*) and flamboyant nouns (*stilt-walkers, fire-eaters, hatchets, saber, rafter, magician, handcuffs, chains*) furnish most of the descriptive color.

The following two passages – the first from a student poetry website, the second from Caliban's speech in Shakespeare's *Tempest* – illustrate two very different attitudes toward *ad*-words:

**Student**: The blackened embers of long dead fires
Of the torches strapped to iron spires
The guard house stands silent, still
The shambled porticulus of broken will
The rotted drawbridge, to the front door
Made of oaken slats, held with iron and ore.

**Shakespeare**: All the infections that the sun sucks up
From bogs, fens, flats, on Prosper fall, and make him
By inch-meal a disease! His spirits hear me,
And yet I needs must curse. But they'll nor pinch,
Fright me with urchin-shows, pitch me i' the mire,
Nor lead me, like a firebrand, in the dark
Out of my way, unless he bid 'em.[33]

Note how eagerly the student poet piles on adjectives, supplying redundant information that we can mostly infer from the accompanying nouns: *blackened* embers, *long dead* fires, *iron* spires, *shambled* porticulus, *broken* will, *rotted* drawbridge, *oaken* slats. In Caliban's complaint, by contrast, vivid verbs (*suck, fall, make, hear, curse, pinch, fright, pitch, lead, bid*) and equally memorable nouns (*infections, sun, bogs, fens, flats, inch-meal, disease, spirits, urchin-shows, mire, firebrand, dark, way*) deliver all the energy and emotion we need.

Journalists can take *ad*-words or leave them, depending on content, context and personal style. But crack open the real estate section of your Sunday newspaper, and you will find adjectives running wild:

Some extra special features like the scullery off the kitchen
are interesting touches which add distinct style. Muted colors,
contemporary "washed" timber floors, split doors, elegant furnishings
and high-quality fittings feature throughout.

This over-the-top advertisement shows us why *ad*-words sometimes earn a bad name among serious writers. Adjectives and adverbs, like nouns, convey either concrete or abstract information: for example, we can picture *muted* colors and imagine stepping through *split* doors, but we cannot see, feel or touch qualities such as *extra special, interesting, distinct, contemporary, elegant* and *high-quality*. The author of the advertisement works hard to persuade us that we will adore this house. Many readers, however, will instinctively distrust any writer who offers only empty platitudes rather than useful facts.

In academic writing, likewise, *ad*-words sometimes supply more clutter than color, more padding than precision:

> Developing an accurate understanding of the multiple factors influencing students' outcomes, and particularly the role of specific community college practices in this process, is crucial if institutional and state leaders seek to improve educational attainment of community college students.[34]

In this excerpt from a higher education research journal, adjectives such as *accurate, multiple, specific, crucial, institutional* and *educational* add up to fairly forgettable prose. Like their "zombie noun" cousins, academic *ad*-words can be recognised by predictable suffixes (*able, ac, al, ant, ary, ent, ful, ible, ic, ive, less, ous*) and a tendency to cannibalize other words (*specify → specific, institute → institution → institutional*). In phrases such as "*secondary* education" or "*constitutional* government," they partner with equally abstract nouns to convey key concepts. But without the addition of visual details and real-life examples, the monotonous rhythms of academic *ad*-words risk lulling your readers to sleep.

Now that you have been persuaded to jettison all *ad*-words from your writing, let's complicate the issue. Imagine Vladimir Nabokov's *Lolita* stripped of its luxurious adjectives:

There are two kinds of *visual* memory: one when you *skillfully* recreate an image in the laboratory of your mind, with your eyes *open* (and then I see Annabel in such *general* terms as: "*honey-colored* skin," "*thin* arms," "*brown bobbed* hair," "*long* lashes," "*big bright* mouth"); and the other when you *instantly* evoke, with *shut* eyes, on the *dark* innerside of your eyelids, the *objective, absolutely optical* replica of a *beloved* face, a *little* ghost in *natural* colors.[35]

Or Romeo's soliloquy in Shakespeare's *Romeo and Juliet* shorn of *ad*-words:

> But *soft*! What light through *yonder* window breaks?
> It is the East, and Juliet is the sun!
> Arise, *fair* sun, and kill the *envious* moon
> Who is *already sick* and *pale* with grief
> That thou her maid art *far more fair* than she.
> Be not her maid, since she is *envious.*
> Her *vestal* livery is but *sick* and *green*,
> And none but fools do wear it.[36]

Or Richard Dawkins' elegant obituary of fellow scientist W. D. Hamilton without its six perfectly placed adverbs:

> An ingenious theory exists, *widely* attributed to an author whom I shall call X. Hamilton and I were once talking termites, and he spoke *favorably* of X's theory. "But Bill," I protested, "That isn't X's theory. It's your theory. You thought of it first." He *gloomily* denied it, so I asked him to wait while I ran to the library. I returned with a bound journal volume and shoved under his nose his own *discreetly* buried paragraph on termites. *Eeyorishly*, he conceded that, yes, it did appear to be his own theory after all, but X had explained it much

better. In a world where scientists vie for priority, Hamilton was *endearingly* unique.[37]

Adverbs such as *gloomily*, *discreetly* and *endearingly* offer insights into Hamilton's character that Dawkins could not easily have communicated using nouns and verbs alone, while the glorious neologism *eeyorishly* speaks volumes not only about Hamilton's personality but also about Dawkins' affection for his deceased colleague. As these examples show, *ad*-words are not necessarily bad words; for some writers, they are as crucial as ink or oxygen.

# Exercises

Are you an *ad*-word addict? The following exercises will help you fine-tune your cravings without forcing you to give up *ad*-words altogether.

### *Ad-ditions and subtractions*

Find any passage jam-packed with *ad*-words, such as this excerpt from John Banville's Booker-Prize-winning novel, *The Sea*:

> The **first** thing I saw of them was their motor car. . . . It was a **low-slung, scarred** and **battered black** model with **beige leather** seats and a **big spoked polished wood steering** wheel. Books with **bleached** and **dog-eared** covers were thrown **carelessly** on the shelf under the **sportily raked back** window.[38]

Highlight all the adjectives and adverbs, including nouns and verbs used as adjectives (*leather* seats, *bleached* covers). What happens when you replace some of the highlighted *ad*-words with new ones: for example, *bleached* and *dog-eared* with *bright* and *colorful*? Could any of the *ad*-words be eliminated without ill effect? Are any of them indispensible?

Rereading the example above, do you find yourself savoring Banville's adjective-rich style, or do you feel his prose suffers from an *ad*-word glut? You can learn a lot about stylish writing from emulating the sentence structures of an author you admire – or, conversely, from avoiding the syntactic habits of a writer whose work you dislike.

### *Adverb alternatives*

Compose a series of sentences in which different adverbs all modify the same verb.

**Examples:**

- She walked **painfully** toward the car.
- She walked **happily** toward the car.
- She walked **drunkenly** toward the car.
- She walked **absent-mindedly** toward the car.

Next, replace each verb-plus-adverb combination with a new, more precise or vivid verb:

**Examples:**

- She **dragged** herself toward the car.
- She **sauntered** toward the car.
- She **stumbled** toward the car.
- She **meandered** toward the car.

What do you gain, and what do you lose, from each transaction?

## Ad-word dump

Clear out your mental cobwebs with an *ad*-word dump:

- On a blank piece of paper, write down every adjective and adverb you can think of.
- Read through your list of *ad*-words and circle all the fresh, unusual ones. Scrap the "academic adjectives" (those ending with the suffixes *able, ac, al, ant, ary, ent, ful, ible, ic, ive, less, ous*) and any adverbs that strike you as pompous or dogmatic (for example *clearly, obviously*). Save the others for a rainy day – but do remember to use them in conjunction with active verbs and concrete nouns, not as substitutes.

# WritersDiet Test example 4

The phenomenon of political crime has been neglected in western criminology, attracting the attention of only a relative handful of scholars. From the 1960s a small number of critical researchers sought to broaden the horizons of criminology, exploring the manner in which much deviant behavior embodied, however inchoately, elements of protest against the prevailing social, moral and political order. Yet other critical scholars switched the focus altogether by concentrating on state crime. The impact of this work on mainstream criminology, however, remained limited and probably diminished as the optimistic climate of radical protest in the 1960s and 1970s gave way to the neo-conservative chill of the Thatcher/Reagan years, the implosion of Soviet communism and the apparent global triumph of western capitalism.

**WritersDiet fitness ratings:**

| | |
|---|---|
| verbs | Lean |
| nouns | Fit & trim |
| prepositions | Needs toning |
| adjectives/adverbs | Heart attack |
| it, this, that, there | Lean |
| **Overall** | **Flabby** |

**Comments:** This extract from a criminology journal contains relatively few *be*-verbs or abstract nouns (a healthy sign of verb-driven, concrete prose) but a high percentage of "academic *ad*-words." Is this adjectival excess a conscious indulgence or an unconscious stylistic tic? If the latter, the author might want to address his *ad*-word addiction.[39]

# 5.

# Waste words

**Key principles in this chapter:**

- Use *it* and *this* only when you can state exactly which noun each word refers to.
- As a general rule, avoid using *that* more than once in a single sentence or three times in a paragraph, except to achieve a specific stylistic effect.
- Beware of sweeping generalizations that begin with "*There*."

The words *it*, *this*, *that* and *there* – collectively referred to in this chapter as "waste words" – function in our language like "bad fat" in our diet. Not only do they supply little verbal nutrition, but their mere presence in a sentence often signals the proximity of other heart-attack-inducing elements such as *be*-verbs, abstract nouns and long strings of prepositions. While waste words can add flavor and texture to any writing, in high doses they can clog up your prose as surely as cholesterol clogs your arteries or grease clogs your sink.

Let's look at *it* first. Employed strategically, this diminutive word wields impressive linguistic power. The original "It Girl," Elinor Glyn, imbued *it* with mystery and sex appeal. In phrases such as "I get *it*" or "*It's* in the bag," *it* equals *everything*. Portia's repetition of *it* in Shakespeare's *Merchant of Venice* lends her speech an incantatory quality, emphasizing the power and holiness of mercy, gentle as rain yet mightier than kings:

> The quality of mercy is not strain'd,
> *It* droppeth as the gentle rain from heaven
> Upon the place beneath: *it* is twice blest;
> *It* blesseth him that gives and him that takes:
> 'Tis mightiest in the mightiest: *it* becomes
> The throned monarch better than his crown . . .[40]

When used as a placeholder for a previously mentioned noun, *it* prevents unnecessary repetition:

> Every time he threw the ball, she caught *it*.

Here, *it* clearly equals *ball*. However, suppose we were to write:

> The girl threw the vase through the window and broke *it*.

What did the girl break: the vase or the window? Because *it* could logically refer either to the first noun after *threw* (vase) or to the noun closest to *broke* (window), we are left to guess the author's meaning.

More serious problems occur when writers employ *it* as a semantic catch-all, a crutch word with no clear referent. Academic authors often display a touching faith in their readers' ability to interpret this kind of nebulous *it*, as in the following excerpt from a book about workplace learning:

> Full participation stands in contrast to only one aspect of the concept
> of peripherality as we see *it*: *It* places the emphasis on what partial
> participation is not, or not yet.[41]

Here, *it* occurs not just once but twice, separated only by a colon. If we
take time to decipher the sentence, we can infer that the first *it* probably refers to "the concept of peripherality" and the second *it* to "full
participation." But how can we be sure? And why should we have to
work so hard? The confusing double *it* acts as the final nail in the coffin
of a sentence already afflicted by a deadly combination of weak verbs
(*stands*, *places*, *is*), abstract nouns (*participation*, *contrast*, *aspect*, *concept*, *peripherality*, *emphasis*) and static prepositions (*in*, *to*, *of*, *on*).

   *It* tends to hang around with *be*-verbs and fellow waste words, especially *that*:

- *It* can *be* shown *that* . . .
- *It is* my position *that* . . .
- We regard *it* as self-evident *that* . . .
- *It* appears *that* . . .
- *It is* a truth universally acknowledged, *that* a single man
  in possession of a good fortune, must *be* in want of a wife.
  (Jane Austen, *Pride and Prejudice*)

It is a point well worth conceding that even the stodgiest *it*-phrase,
in the hands of a writer as clever as Jane Austen, can score rhetorical
points. Some writers even exploit *its* ambiguity, as Vietnam veteran
Yusef Komunyakaa does with the title of his poem "Facing It," which
alludes both to the poet's physical act of facing the Vietnam War
Memorial in Washington, D.C. – a wall of reflective granite carved
with the names of all the American soldiers who died in the war –
and to his metaphorical act of facing his own past. As a general rule,

however, unless you can state exactly what noun this insipid little pronoun refers to, it may be best to avoid the temptation of sprinkling your prose with *it*.

*This*, like *it*, pulls its own weight in many grammatical situations. Together with its siblings *these*, *those* and *that*, *this* can direct a reader's attention to a specific object or idea:

- I'm catching *this* bus today, but I caught *that* one yesterday.
- Do you like *this* dress?
- I want to buy *this* television.

As long as you can name the noun that *this* refers to, you stand on firm rhetorical ground. All too frequently, however, *this* becomes a cover-up for fuzzy thinking. Writers of academic prose excel at exploiting the ambiguous *this*:

MRCD [Multirecursive Constraint Demotion] can be applied to a set of full structural descriptions, and it will either determine that the set is inconsistent or return a grammar consistent with all of the descriptions. *This* means that we could try to deal with structural ambiguity by collecting a set of overt forms, and for each overt form generate all possible interpretations of the form.[42]

Here, *this* serves as shorthand for "the fact that MRCD can be applied to a set of full structural descriptions," or perhaps for "the fact that MRCD will either determine that the set is inconsistent or return a grammar consistent with all of the descriptions." No wonder the author – ironically, a linguist – has dumped *this* into the paragraph and fled, rather than taking the trouble to state his argument clearly and concisely.

Whenever you encounter *this* on its own, ask yourself, "This *what*?" *This* concept, *this* principle, *this* statement?

Her watercolors were not simply beautiful pieces of art, but also didactic objects that bore the burden of teaching others about Spiritualism and sharing the spirits' lessons about the nature of God. *This* was a lot to ask of works whose non-objective imagery could make them seem impenetrable.[43]

This *what* was a lot to ask?

The democratic troubles in Bolivia and the Andean region more broadly can partly be read as a reaction against the established political class in each country. *This* has good and bad implications.[44]

This *what* has good and bad implications? The fact that the democratic troubles in Bolivia and the Andean region can be read as a reaction against the established political class in each country? The fact that the democratic troubles in Bolivia and the Andean region *are* a reaction against the established political class in each country? Here, *this* functions like a cloak tossed over a puddle to disguise muddy thinking.

And yet, as always, there are some compelling exceptions to the rule: authors who use the ambiguous *this* to fine effect. In a passage from Shakespeare's *Twelfth Night*, for example, Fabian berates a jealous Sir Andrew Aguecheek:

She did show favor to the youth in your sight only to exasperate you, to awaken your dormouse valour, to put fire in your heart, and brimstone in your liver. You should then have accosted her, and with some excellent jests, fire-new from the mint, you should have banged the youth into dumbness. *This* was looked for at your hand, and ***this*** was balked: the double gilt of ***this*** opportunity you let time wash off, and now you are sailed into the north of my lady's opinion, where you will hang like an icicle on a Dutchman's beard . . .[45]

Shakespeare's double *this* ("*This* was looked for at your hand, and *this* was balked") encompasses all the actions on Fabian's list: becoming exasperated and valorous and angry; declaring passion to the lady; telling jokes to shame and silence the rival; seizing a golden opportunity to act. This *what* was looked for? This response, this resolve, and more. In a passage crammed chock-full of concrete nouns, active verbs and vivid imagery, Shakespeare can afford to indulge in a moment of strategic ambiguity.

*That*, like *this*, seldom causes problems when accompanied by a noun. Indeed, when deployed as a determiner – a specifically slanted variant of *the* – *that* performs yeoman service: *That Girl; That '70s Show; That Darn Cat!* When W. B. Yeats opens his poem "Sailing to Byzantium" with the phrase, "*That* is no country for old men," he points to a land far far away, in the realm of the imagination: *that* country, not *this* one. Even ambiguous phrases such as *That's great!* and *What's that?* can make perfect sense in the appropriate context.

When used as a link between clauses, however, *that* risks becoming as unhealthy as a pat of butter on a frosted cupcake. The following passage aptly defines the linguistic phenomenon of *logorrhoea* as "prose that is highly abstract and contains little concrete language":

> Writers in academic fields *that* concern themselves mostly with the abstract, such as philosophy and especially postmodernism, often fail to include extensive concrete examples of their ideas. . . . The widespread expectation *that* scholarly works in these fields will look at first glance like nonsense is the source of humor *that* pokes fun at these fields by comparing actual nonsense with real academic writing.[46]

Note how each of the first two *that*-clauses drives a wedge between a sentence's subject and its verb: seventeen words separate *writers* and *fail*, and thirteen words intervene between *expectation* and *is*. In this example, with its pudgy prepositional phrases and abstract nouns, *that* serves as a symptom rather than a cause of flabby writing. Authors of lean prose employ *that* too, of course, but in moderation and with a clear sense of purpose.

Like *that*, the word *there* possesses both a light side and a dark side. Together with its siblings *here* and *where*, *there* positions us in the world: "Are we *there* yet?" "Will you go *there* again tomorrow?" Sometimes, however, *there* loses its sense of place and becomes a catch-all word meaning "the universe contains" or "one can surmise the existence of." In a sentence such as "*There* used to be more friendly people in the world than *there* are now," what does *there* actually mean?

The universal *there* usually dances cheek to cheek with *be*-verbs:

- *There are* many reasons why . . .
- *There is* a rule that . . .
- *There* could *be* no better way to . . .
- *Are there* any alternatives?

Gertrude Stein's famous aphorism about Oakland, California – "*There* is no *there there*" – plays with the potential double meaning of *there*. Even while commenting humorously on the relationship of grammar to geography, Stein offers us a warning: when you open a sentence with "*There is*," there is sometimes no substance there.

Should you avoid the universal *there* entirely? Of course not. In the works of skillful writers such as Shakespeare or Emily Dickinson, *there*-clauses lend emphasis and weight to the nouns they introduce:

- *There* was speech in their dumbness, language in their very gesture.[47]
- *There* is another sky,
  Ever serene and fair,

And *there* is another sunshine,
Though it be darkness *there*.[48]

However, writers of academic prose await a flabby fate if they fail to hold *there* in check:

> With most or even all vague predicates, *it* soon appears *that* the idea *that there* is a sharp division between the positive cases and the borderline ones, and between the borderline cases and the negative ones, can no more be sustained than can the idea *that there* is a sharp division between negative and positive ones.[49]

In this excerpt from a philosophical essay aptly titled "Is There Higher-Order Vagueness?" *there* joins with several partners in crime – *it, that* and *be*-verbs – to produce a sentence of almost unfathomable, and by no means higher-order, obscurity. This leads us to the conclusion that there really is no excuse for it when an academic writes quite as confusingly as that.

In the following sentences composed by undergraduate writers, the words *it, this, that* and *there* (and occasionally *what*) all congregate together, pulling *be*-verbs, abstract nouns and prepositional phrases into their orbit:

- *This* essay will consist of information about nine composers and one piece of work *that* each of them is known for.
- *There* are a number of studies *that* show *that* if a cellular phone is being used near a cardiac pacemaker, *it* causes interference.
- *It* is interesting *that* so many people believe in aliens, given *that there* is no actual proof of their existence.
- *What* is most striking about *this* photograph is *that it* is not really an accurate depiction of real life.

But who can blame these students for padding their paragraphs with "waste words"? Many of their teachers – the best brains in the business – do exactly the same thing. The excerpts below come from academic publications in the fields of general science, sociology, philosophy and literary studies, respectively:

- [Science] What does *it* take to establish *that* such incompleteness will actually occur in a specific system? The basic way to do *it* is to show *that* the system is universal.[50]
- [Sociology] *It* is important to recognize *that* sex segregation is a multifaceted and complicated phenomenon *that* is difficult to aggregate into one single index of sex segregation.[51]
- [Philosophy] A major consequence of all *this*, then, is *that* when language does appear, semantics (*that* is, meaning) is already anchored in *this* bodily conceptuality. In short, *there* exists a universal core of signifiers *that* have a natural relationship to signifieds.[52]
- [Literary studies] Is *it* the case *that* recognition consists, as *it* does for Hegel, in a reciprocal act whereby I recognize *that* the Other is structured in the same way *that* I am, and I recognize *that* the Other also makes, or can make, *this* very recognition of sameness?[53]

If you consider such convoluted sentences to be unavoidable in academic writing, take a look at these four passages written by scholars from a similar range of disciplines:

- [Science] Today as never before, the sky is menacing. . . . Even in daytime, reflected light on a floating dandelion seed, or a spider riding a wisp of gossamer in the sun's eye can bring excited questions from the novice unused to estimating the distance or nature of aerial objects.[54]

- [History] Farmers make their living by slightly altering nature to achieve human ends. . . . In short, the farmers' metier has everything to do with flows of energy through ecosystems, fluxes of hydrology, and the invisible transference of nitrogen from air to soil and back again.[55]
- [Philosophy] We live in deceptive times. . . . Lies and other forms of deceptive behavior degrade our characters, unravel the fabric of civil society, and threaten our progress toward the good life.[56]
- [Literary studies] We tend today to think of *Jane Eyre* as moral gothic, "myth domesticated," *Pamela*'s daughter and *Rebecca*'s aunt, the archetypal scenario for all those mildly thrilling romantic encounters between a scowling Byronic hero (who owns a gloomy mansion) and a trembling heroine (who can't quite figure out the mansion's floor plan).[57]

Rich in concrete nouns and active verbs, with not a "waste word" in sight, these examples prove that academic writers can indeed communicate complex ideas in language we take pleasure in reading.

# Exercises

### *Shake it out*

In a sample of your own writing or a piece of published academic prose, highlight every occurrence of the word *it*:

> **Example:** Many writers find **it** all too tempting to use this little pronoun as liberally as if **it** were a more interesting vocabulary item than **it** really is.

What is *it* doing in the above sentence? The first *it* ("Many writers find *it* all too tempting") is catchy but defies definition; we cannot clearly say what *it* stands for. The second *it* refers unambiguously to the most recent noun, *pronoun*; but why, we might wonder, does *it* occur twice in a row with two different meanings? The third *it*, like the second, refers to *pronoun*; however, a new noun, *item*, has shown up to sow additional confusion. An alert editor would probably opt to retain just one *it* (the first or second) and scuttle the other two.

### *Analyze this*

Now try the same exercise with *this*.

> **Example:** When we use **this** word too frequently, we grow lazy and complacent. **This** causes us to lose sight of our own meaning. How can we prevent **this** from happening?

Here, only the first *this* accompanies a noun ("*this word*"); the second and third *this*es have no clear referent. If you cannot easily answer the "this *what*?" question, consider rephrasing your sentence to omit the ambiguous *this*.

### *That's no good*

Whenever you find yourself using *that* more than once in a single sentence or more than three or four times in a paragraph, ask yourself a simple question: Do all those *that*-phrases direct the flow of your sentences, or do they muddy the waters?

#### **Examples:**

· We hold these truths to be self-evident, **that** all men are created equal, **that** they are endowed by their Creator with certain unalienable Rights, **that** among these are Life, Liberty and the pursuit of Happiness.
· A sentence **that** makes clear **that** the author has not thought carefully about its structure will ensure **that** readers lose their way.

In the first example, from the opening lines of the United States Declaration of Independence, parallel *that*-phrases guide us neatly through a series of parallel ideas. In the second example, by contrast, the repeated *that*s confuse rather than clarify, signaling a lack of authorial attention and care.

Do not be tempted, by the way, to reduce your *that*-quota simply by replacing *that* with *which*. Grammar mavens note a crucial distinction between the two words:

· The dog **that** bit the child had very sharp teeth.
· The cat, **which** disliked children, purred loudly.

A *that*-phrase that directly follows a noun ("the dog *that* bit the child") provides us with essential information about the noun, whereas a *which*-phrase, which is normally set off by commas, remains grammatically expendable and can be deleted without ill effect.

### Getting over there

There is no reason why you should not use the word *there* from time to time. Indeed, if there were a law passed tomorrow banning all use of the word *there* except as a marker of place, there would undoubtedly be protests by professional writers.

The paragraph above contains three *there*-phrases (not counting "the word *there*"):

**There** is no reason why you should not use the word *there* at least occasionally. Indeed, if **there** were a law passed tomorrow banning all use of the word *there* except as a marker of place, **there** would undoubtedly be protests by professional writers.

Let's leave the opening *there* alone but eliminate the other two:

**There** is no reason why you should not use the word *there* at least occasionally. Indeed, if a law were passed tomorrow banning all use of the word *there* except as a marker of place, professional writers would undoubtedly protest.

With no significant loss of meaning, we have trimmed the second sentence from 44 words down to 40 (a lard factor of 10%).

Try writing a few sentences crammed with "waste words": e.g. "There is a belief that difficult assignments are unfair." Easy, right? Now rephrase your sentences to eliminate, say, half the "waste words" and forms of *be*: for example "Many people resent difficult assignments." Like a hard workout at the gym, this exercise requires considerable effort. You might even have to repeat your exertion every time you write something new. Persevere! Your prose will become leaner and sharper, and your readers will thank you.

# WritersDiet Test example 5

Full participation, however, stands in contrast to only one aspect of the concept of peripherality as we see it: It places the emphasis on what partial participation is not, or not yet. In our usage, *peripherality* is also a *positive* term, whose most salient conceptual antonyms are *unrelatedness* or *irrelevance* to ongoing activity. The partial participation of newcomers is by no means "disconnected" from the practice of interest. Furthermore, it is also a dynamic concept. In this sense, peripherality, when it is enabled, suggests an opening, a way of gaining access to sources for understanding through growing involvement. The ambiguity inherent in peripheral participation must then be connected to issues of legitimacy, of the social organization of and control over resources, if it is to gain its full analytical potential.

---

**WritersDiet fitness ratings:**

| | |
|---|---|
| verbs | Heart attack |
| nouns | Heart attack |
| prepositions | Flabby |
| adjectives/adverbs | Needs toning |
| it, this, that, there | Flabby |
| **Overall** | **Heart attack** |

---

**Comments:** This relentlessly abstract passage contains virtually no concrete language. Uninspiring verbs – *stands*, *places*, *suggests* – contribute little energy to sentences already weighed down by prepositional phrases, multiple *be*-verbs, ambiguous *its* and all those zombie nouns.[58]

# AFTERWORD: HEALTHY WRITING

If a diet and exercise regimen deprives you of the foods you love and forces you to perform physical exercises you hate, you will almost certainly abandon it eventually. Effective fitness programs promise no quick fix to render you fit and trim; instead, they inspire gradual, lasting change. The Writer's Diet follows a similar philosophy. If you successfully edit one piece of writing but then return to your old habits the next time you compose something new, your prose style will end up no better off than before. The trick is to transform not only the way you write but the way you think about writing.

Nutritionists warn us to shun chips, candy bars, soda and other food items that contain mostly "empty calories." But how can we resist their addictive flavor and easy abundance? Likewise, e-mails, text messages, blog posts and other "new media" encourage us to write hastily, junkily, without regard to quality. The good news is that, in a digital culture where teachers bemoan their students' illiteracy, young people are writing more prolifically than ever before. The bad news is that, just as pretzels and potato chips can dull our appetite for smoked salmon and fresh blueberries, "junk prose" can dull our sensitivity to elegant language.

So how do we avoid the temptations of rubbishy prose? We can start by attending to the *quality* of the writing we produce and consume each day. Proponents of the international "Slow Food" movement urge you to buy your vegetables fresh from the farmer's market, prepare them thoughtfully, cook them slowly and savor your meals with loved ones. Similarly, you can maintain your taste for fresh, flavorful writing by balancing junk prose with words that count.

You can also improve your writing by striving for *variety*. Just as famous chefs love to dine out in other chefs' restaurants, accomplished authors relish the work of other masters of the game. To expand your verbal repertoire, read widely and attentively in fields outside your own range of expertise. What can you learn from analyzing a favorite author's sentences? What happens when you vary the length and syntax of your own, or throw in a new vocabulary word, or experiment with metaphor and analogy?

Finally, remember to take *pleasure* in your writing. You need not waste time obsessing about the grammar in your outgoing e-mails; sometimes it's okay to let junk food be junk food. Nor should you realistically expect that cranking out an overdue academic article or term paper will transport you into a state of rapture. But why not take time, at least occasionally, to revel in the written word? Compose a love letter. Craft a haiku text message. Send a hand-written note to a friend. Not only will your writing improve; so, quite possibly, will the quality of your life.

# WritersDiet Test example 6

Shakespeare's plays show us how a single author can experiment with a range of stylistic flourishes.

### Be-verbs

I will be master of what is mine own:
She is my goods, my chattels; she is my house . . .

### Nominalizations

I crave fit disposition for my wife.
Due reference of place and exhibition,
With such accommodation and besort
As levels with her breeding.

### Prepositions

So, at his sight, away his fellows fly;
And, at our stamp, here o'er and o'er one falls;
He murder cries and help from Athens calls.

### Ad-dictions *

Pity, you ancient stones, those tender babes
Whom envy hath immured within your walls!
Rough cradle for such little pretty ones!
Rude ragged nurse, old sullen playfellow
For tender princes, use my babies well!

### Waste words

For in that sleep of death what dreams may come
When we have shuffled off this mortal coil,
Must give us pause: there's the respect
That makes calamity of so long life . . .[59]

---

* Note that most of the adjectives highlighted here would not be counted by the WritersDiet Test, which searches only for "academic *ad*-words."

# APPENDIX: THE WRITERSDIET TEST

You can take the WritersDiet Test online at www.writersdiet.com, or you can perform the test manually with a colored highlighter. Based on a simple algorithm, the test calculates the "fitness" of your writing in each of five grammatical categories. The higher the percentage of highlighted words in each category, the "flabbier" your diagnosis, which can be interpreted as follows:

| | |
|---|---|
| *Lean* | Fat-free prose |
| *Fit & trim* | In excellent condition |
| *Needs toning* | Would benefit from a light workout |
| *Flabby* | Judicious editing required |
| *Heart attack* | May call for editorial liposuction! |

The WritersDiet Test prompts you to think about *how*, *why* and *how often* you use the highlighted words; however, you are not expected to delete them all or banish them completely. You might even decide, in the end, to make no changes at all. The "mirror, mind and zipper" test imparts far more useful information than a measuring tape or bathroom scale ever could. Do you look good? Do you feel good? Do your words fit you well?

The WritersDiet Test offers a diagnosis, not a prescription; a pair of tinted glasses, not a magic bullet. It is up to you to make intelligent use of the targeted feedback the test provides. Sentences, like people, come in many shapes and sizes, and the world would become a very boring place indeed if we all wrote – or looked – exactly the same way!

# WritersDiet Test Instructions (manual version)

Select a sample of your writing and excerpt a passage of exactly **100 words**, not including citations and quotations. Do not worry if the passage finishes mid-sentence. Highlight your text as follows:

- **Verbs:** With an orange pencil, highlight all the **be-verbs**: *am*, *is*, *are*, *was*, *were*, *be*, *being*, *been*.
- **Nouns:** With a blue pencil, highlight all the **nouns** that end with the following suffixes: *ion*, *ism*, *ty*, *ment*, *ness*, *ance* or *ence*.
  - Include plurals (*occurrences*) and nouns used as adjectives (*precision* tool).
  - Do not include proper nouns (*Felicity*, *Namibia*) or nouns not rooted in an adjective or verb (*prism*, *city*, *dance*).
- **Prepositions:** With a green pencil, highlight all the **prepositions** in your writing sample: *about*, *above*, *across*, *after*, *against*, *along*, *among*, *around*, *at*, *before*, *behind*, *below*, *beneath*, *beside*, *between*, *beyond*, *by*, *down*, *during*, *for*, *from*, *in*, *inside*, *into*, *like*, *near*, *of*, *off*, *on*, *onto*, *out*, *outside*, *over*, *past*, *since*, *through*, *throughout*, *till*, *to*, *toward*, *under*, *underneath*, *until*, *up*, *upon*, *with*, *within*, *without*.
  - Highlight *to* even when it occurs as part of an infinitive verb construction, e.g., "*to* run."
  - When two prepositions occur together ("He got *up from* the sofa"), count them separately.
- **Ad-words:** With a yellow pencil, highlight all the **adjectives** and **adverbs** that end with the following suffixes: *able*, *ac*, *al*, *ant*, *ary*, *ent*, *ful*, *ible*, *ic*, *ive*, *less*, *ous*.
- **"Waste words":** With a pink pencil, highlight the words *it*, *this*, *that* and *there*.

Now calculate your individual fitness ratings for each category and determine your overall fitness rating:

- **Count** your highlighted words and record this in the appropriate box in each of the five columns here:

| BLANK SCORING CHART (100 WORDS) | | | | | |
|---|---|---|---|---|---|
| **Verbs** | **Nouns** | **Prepositions** | **Ad-words** | **Waste words** | **FITNESS RATING** |
| ‹3 | ‹4 | ‹14 | ‹6 | ‹3 | Lean |
| 3 | 4 | 14–15 | 6–7 | 3 | Fit & trim |
| 4 | 5 | 16–17 | 8–9 | 4 | Needs toning |
| 5 | 6 | 18–19 | 10–11 | 5 | Flabby |
| 6+ | 7+ | 20+ | 12+ | 6+ | Heart attack |

- **Read across** to the Fitness rating column to find your ratings for each category, and note these in the chart below.
- **Assign** a scoring value for each of your five individual ratings: Lean = 1; Fit & trim = 2; Needs toning = 4; Flabby = 16; Heart attack = 32.
- **Add** the five values to find your total score. This will determine your Overall fitness rating. Total scores of 5–7 = Lean; 8–11 = Fit & trim; 12–23 = Needs toning; 24–63 = Flabby; 64+ = Heart attack.

| OVERALL FITNESS RATING CALCULATION | | |
|---|---|---|
| **CATEGORY** | **FITNESS RATING** | **SCORE** |
| **Verbs** | | |
| **Nouns** | | |
| **Prepositions** | | |
| **Ad-words** | | |
| **Waste words** | | |
| TOTAL SCORE | | |
| OVERALL FITNESS RATING | | |

# WritersDiet Test example 7

Scholars have also spilled a great deal of ink to demonstrate how a lack of unity may contribute to a social movement organization's failure or collapse, and numerous empirical studies suggest that division can lead to the collapse of an organization or a structural coalition. Yet not all organizations fall apart because of internal division. Given the size and longevity of NOW, it provides an apt case for examining how organizations withstand internal differences. Sociologist Jo Reger, for example, uses the case of the New York City chapter of NOW to suggest that an organization can develop multiple and varying . . .[60]

| | | | SCORING CHART EXAMPLE 7 | | | |
|---|---|---|---|---|---|---|
| **Verbs** | **Nouns** | **Prepositions** | **Ad-words** | **Waste words** | **FITNESS RATING** | |
| <3 | <4 | <14 | <6 | <3 | **Lean** | |
| 3 | 4 | 14–15 | 6–7 | 3 | **Fit & trim** | |
| 4 | 5 | 16–17 | 8–9 | 4 | **Needs toning** | |
| 5 | 6 | 18–19 | 10–11 | 5 | **Flabby** | |
| 6+ | 7+ | 20+ | 12+ | 6+ | **Heart attack** | |

- **Find** the five individual fitness ratings for Example 7 by using the Scoring chart.
- **Assign** the correct value to each of the individual ratings: Lean = 1; Fit & trim = 2; Needs toning = 4; Flabby = 16; Heart attack = 32.
- **Add** the five values to find a total score for Example 7. This will determine the Overall fitness rating. Total scores of 5–7 = Lean; 8–11 = Fit & trim; 12–23 = Needs toning; 24–63 = Flabby; 64+ = Heart attack.

| OVERALL FITNESS RATING EXAMPLE 7 | | |
|---|---|---|
| **CATEGORY** | **FITNESS RATING** | **SCORE** |
| **Verbs** | Lean | 1 |
| **Nouns** | Heart attack | 32 |
| **Prepositions** | Lean | 1 |
| **Ad-words** | Fit & trim | 2 |
| **Waste words** | Fit & trim | 2 |
| | **TOTAL SCORE** | **38** |
| | **OVERALL FITNESS RATING** | **Flabby** |

**Comments:** This 100-word excerpt from the *Journal of the History of Sexuality* scores "Lean" or "Fit & trim" in four out of five categories. However, the passage earns a "heart attack" rating in the Nouns category and thus a "Flabby" Overall rating (1 + 1 + 2 + 2 + 32 = 38). The opening phrase, "Scholars have spilled a great deal of ink," supplies the only concrete detail in an otherwise abstract passage. The author might consider reducing the high number of "zombie nouns" (12) and adding more concrete language.

# WritersDiet Test Instructions (electronic version)

Select a recent sample of your own writing: a finished, polished piece of prose that, in your opinion, represents your work at its best.

Go to the WritersDiet website (**www.writersdiet.com**) and cut and paste a 100- to 1000-word extract from your writing sample into the text box. Shorter excerpts (100–500 words) work best for targeting specific paragraphs; longer samples (500–1000 words) give more of a "big picture" view and can help you spot recurring patterns in your writing.

- **Click** "Run the test." Your words will light up in color, and you will see an individual "WritersDiet fitness rating" for each of the five word categories, as well as an overall rating.
- **To save** your results as a downloadable pdf, click "See full diagnosis."
- **To run** the test again, click "Test new sample."

For best results:

- **Fine-tune** your diagnosis by clicking the Advanced tab on the text box and trying out the different options.
- **Read** all the information on the website carefully, especially the Frequently Asked Questions (FAQs).
- **Test** a variety of samples to get a feel for the test before making adjustments to specific passages.

# WritersDiet Test example 8

Fourscore and seven years ago our fathers brought forth on this continent, a new nation, conceived in Liberty, and dedicated to the proposition that all men are created equal. Now we are engaged in a great civil war, testing whether that nation, or any nation so conceived and so dedicated, can long endure. We are met on a great battle-field of that war. We have come to dedicate a portion of that field, as a final resting place for those who here gave their lives that that nation might live . . .

---

**WritersDiet fitness ratings (for the full speech):**

| | |
|---|---|
| verbs | Fit & trim |
| nouns | Fit & trim |
| prepositions | Lean |
| adjectives/adverbs | Lean |
| it, this, that, there | Heart attack |
| **Overall** | **Flabby** |

---

**Comments:** If Abraham Lincoln had carried a laptop computer with wifi access on the train to Gettysburg, he might have pasted the 269 words of his hastily written speech into the WritersDiet Test and noticed a few verbal tics: the double *that*, the repeated *it*s. Would he then have tweaked his "Flabby" text to make it "Fit & trim"? Maybe, maybe not. As a politician, Lincoln would no doubt have understood that a feedback tool designed mainly for academic writers will not necessarily apply to speechwriting. And as an experienced rhetorician, he would have had the self-confidence to make his own decisions rather than relying on the advice of an automated computer program.

# REFERENCES

All examples of student writing in this book come from open-access internet sites such as www.directessays.com. All otherwise uncredited examples were composed by the author.

1   Richard Lanham, *Revising Prose*, Third Edition (New York: Macmillan, 1992), 4.
2   Charles Dickens, *A Tale of Two Cities*, Chapter 1.
3   William Shakespeare, *Hamlet*, Act III, Scene 1.
4   John McPhee, "The Founding Fish," *The New York Times*, 8 December 2002.
5   R. Fagin, "Inverting Schema Mappings," *ACM Transactions on Database Systems* 32.4, Article 25 (November 2007): 1.
6   Mickael Le Gac et al, "Phylogenetic Evidence of Host-specific Cryptic Species in the Anther Smut Fungus," *Evolution* 61.1 (2007): 15.
7   Panagiotis G. Ipeirotis et al, "Towards a Query Optimizer for Text-centric Tasks," *ACM Transactions on Database Systems* 32.4, Article 21 (November 2007): 2.
8   Richard Leschen and Thomas Buckley, "Multistate Characters and Diet Shifts: Evolution of Erotylidae (Coleoptera)," *Systematic Biology* 56.1 (2007): 97.
9   Claudia Lapping, "Recodifications of Academic Positions and Reiterations of Desire: Change but Continuity in Gendered Subjectivities," *Studies in Higher Education* 31:4 (2006): 423.
10  Robert Morgan, *Sigodlin* (Middletown, CT: Wesleyan University Press, 1990), 58. Quoted by permission of the author.
11  Kathryn A. Becker-Blease et al, "A Genetic Analysis of Individual Differences in Dissociative Behaviors in Childhood and Adolescence," *Journal of Child Psychology and Psychiatry* 45.3 (March 2004): 522.
12  Alison Gopnik, *The Philosophical Baby: What Children's Minds Tell Us About Truth, Love, and the Meaning of Life* (New York: Farrar, Straus and Giroux, 2009), 50, 53.
13  Emily Dickinson, Poem 254, in *The Complete Poems of Emily Dickinson*, ed. Thomas H. Johnson (Boston: Little, Brown, 1960), 116.
14  A. S. Byatt, *Possession: A Romance* (New York: Vintage, 1991), 63.
15  Dava Sobel, *Longitude* (New York: Penguin, 1996), 4–5.
16  Helen Sword, "Zombie Nouns," *The New York Times*, 23 July 2012.
17  Lori A. Fidler and J. David Johnson, "Communication and Innovation Implementation," *Academy of Management Review* 9.4 (1984): 704.
18  William Shakespeare, *A Midsummer Night's Dream*, Act V, Scene 1.
19  George Smoot, "Looking for the Big Bang," in *Galileo's Commandment: An*

*Anthology of Great Science Writing*, ed. Edmund Blair Bolles (London: Little, Brown, 1999), 239–40.

20 Kwame Anthony Appiah, *Cosmopolitanism: Ethics in a World of Strangers* (New York: Norton, 2006), xi.

21 Joan Didion, "On Self-Respect," in *Slouching Towards Bethlehem* (London: Andre Deutsch, 1969), 143–44.

22 Gary Younge, *The Speech: The Story Behind Dr. Martin Luther King Jr.'s Dream* (Chicago: Haymarket Books, 2013), 118.

23 Anne Salmond, *The Trial of the Cannibal Dog: Captain Cook in the South Seas* (London: Penguin, 2003), xix–xx.

24 Robert N. Proctor, "'-Logos,' '-Ismos,' and '-Ikos': The Political Iconicity of Denominative Suffixes in Science (or, Phonesthemic Tints and Taints in the Coining of Science Domain Names)," *Isis* 98:2 (2007): 290.

25 Lanham, *op. cit.*, 5.

26 Benjamin Robinson, "Socialism's Other Modernity: Quality, Quantity and the Measure of the Human," *Modernism/Modernity* 10.4 (2003): 709.

27 Michele Leggott, "milk and honey taken far far away (ii)," in *Milk & Honey* (Auckland: Auckland University Press, 2005), 44. Quoted by permission of the author.

28 Michele Leggott, "27," in *Like This?* (Christchurch: Caxton Press, 1988), 27. Quoted by permission of the author.

29 Renée Riese Hubert and Judd D. Hubert, "Reading Gertrude Stein in the Light of the Book Artists," *Modernism/Modernity* 10.4 (2003): 683.

30 Claire Colebrook, "The Sense of Space: On the Specificity of Affect in Deleuze and Guattari," *Postmodern Culture* 15.1 (2004): par. 2.

31 Adalaide Morris, *How to Live/What to Do: H.D.'s Cultural Poetics* (Urbana: University of Illinois Press, 2003), 79.

32 Glen David Gold, *Carter Beats the Devil* (New York: Hyperion, 2001), 91.

33 William Shakespeare, *The Tempest*, Act II, Scene 2.

34 Josipa Roksa, "Does the Vocational Focus of Community Colleges Hinder Students' Educational Attainment?" *Review of Higher Education* 29.4 (2006): 499.

35 Vladimir Nabokov, *Lolita* (New York: Berkley Books, 1977), 14.

36 William Shakespeare, *Romeo and Juliet*, Act II, Scene 2.

37 Richard Dawkins, obituary for W. D. Hamilton, in *The Independent*, 3 October 2000.

38 John Banville, *The Sea* (London: Picador, 2005), 6.

39 Russell Hogg, "Criminology, Crime and Politics Before and After 9/11," *Australian and New Zealand Journal of Criminology* 40:1 (2007): 83.

40 William Shakespeare, *The Merchant of Venice*, Act VI, Scene 1.

41 Jean Lave and Etienne Wenger, *Situated Learning: Legitimate Peripheral Participation* (Cambridge: Cambridge University Press, 1991), 35.

42 Bruce Tesar, "Using Inconsistency Detection to Overcome Structural Ambiguity," *Linguistic Inquiry* 35.2 (2004): 231.

43 Rachel Oberter, "Esoteric Art Confronting the Public Eye: The Abstract Spirit Drawings of Georgiana Houghton," *Victorian Studies* 48.2 (2005): 223.

## REFERENCES

44 "High Anxiety in the Andes," *Journal of Democracy* 12.2 (2001): 5. Unsigned editorial.

45 William Shakespeare, *Twelfth Night*, Act III, Scene 2.

46 http://en.wikipedia.org/wiki/Logorrhoea; accessed March 2007. (This entry has since been revised, and the quoted passage has disappeared.)

47 William Shakespeare, *The Winter's Tale*, Act V, Scene 2.

48 Emily Dickinson, Poem 2, in *The Complete Poems of Emily Dickinson*, ed. Thomas H. Johnson (Boston: Little, Brown, 1960), 4.

49 Mark Sainsbury, "Is There Higher-Order Vagueness?" *Philosophical Quarterly* 41.163 (1991): 168.

50 Stephen Wolfram, *A New Kind of Science* (Champaign: Wolfram Media, 2002), 784.

51 Margarita Estévez-Abe, "Gender Bias in Skills and Social Policies: The Varieties of Capitalism Perspective on Sex Segregation," *Social Politics: International Studies in Gender, State and Society* 12.2 (2005): 184.

52 Tony Jackson, "Writing and the Disembodiment of Language," *Philosophy and Literature* 27.1 (2003): 117–18.

53 Judith Butler, "Giving an Account of Oneself," *Diacritics* 31.4 (2001): 22–23.

54 Loren C. Eiseley, "Little Men and Flying Saucers," *Harper's* 206.1234 (March 1953): 86.

55 Geoff Cunfer, "Manure Matters on the Great Plains Frontier," *Journal of Interdisciplinary History* 34.4 (2004): 539.

56 Jeff Karon, "Deception and Intentional Transparency: The Case of Writing," *Philosophy and Literature* 27.1 (2003): 134.

57 Sandra M. Gilbert and Susan Gubar, *The Madwoman in the Attic: The Woman Writer and the Nineteenth-Century Literary Imagination* (New Haven: Yale University Press, 1979), 337.

58 Lave and Wenger, *op. cit.*, 35.

59 William Shakespeare, *The Taming of the Shrew*, Act III, Scene 2; *Othello*, Act I, Scene 3; *A Midsummer Night's Dream*, Act III, Scene 2; *Richard III*, Act IV, Scene 1; *Hamlet*, Act III, Scene 1.

60 Stephanie Gilmore and Elizabeth Kaminski, "A Part and Apart: Lesbian and Straight Feminist Activists Negotiate Identity in a Second-Wave Organization," *Journal of the History of Sexuality* 16:1 (2007): 99.

# INDEX

abstract language, 17–23, 26–27

*ad*-words, *see* adjectives; adverbs

adjectives: "academic adjectives," 16, 28, 39, 43, 47, 48; concrete or abstract, 43; excessive use of, 39–44; derived from nouns or verbs, 22, 26, 43; nouns or verbs used as, 7, 26, 46–47

adverbs: concrete or abstract, 43; excessive use of, 39–48

Appiah, Kwame Anthony, 23–24

Austen, Jane, 51

Banville, John, 46

*be*-verbs, *see* verbs

Byatt, A. S., 20

Churchill, Winston, 35

concrete language, 23–25

Dawkins, Richard, 44–45

Dickens, Charles, 8–9

Dickinson, Emily, 55

Didion, Joan, 24

Gold, Glen David, 41

Hamilton, W. D., 44–45

imagery, 10, 16–20, 23–24, 27, 32, 54

"it," 49–52, 56–58, 59

jargon, 2, 22

King, Martin Luther, 24–25

Lanham, Richard A., 8, 30

lard factor, 8, 13, 23, 61

Leggott, Michele, 32

McPhee, John, 10–11

metaphor, 9, 11–13, 21–23, 31

Morgan, Robert, 18

Morris, Adalaide, 38

Nabokov, Vladimir, 43–44

nominalizations, 17, 21–22, 24–26

nouns: abstract nouns, 17–22, 26–27, 31; concrete nouns, 17–23, 26–27, 38–40; separation from verbs, 29, 34, 36–37

prepositions: effect on syntax, 31–34; dynamic versus static, 31–32, 36; excessive or insufficient use of, 33–35, 38

prepositional phrases, 55–56

sentence length, 30, 33–34

Shakespeare, William, 9–10, 23, 41–42, 44, 50, 53, 55, 65

Smoot, George, 23

Sobel, Dava, 20–21

subject, 13, 14, 33–37, 54

syntax, 5–6, 11–12, 14–15, 34, 64

"that," 54–58, 60

"there," 55–58, 61

"this," 52–54, 56–59

verbs: active verbs, 1–3, 5–12, 14–15, 39–40; *be*-verbs, 5–9, 12, 49–51, 55–56; passive verb constructions, 6, 14–15; separation from nouns, 29, 34, 36–37; use as adjectives, 7, 46; use in vivid prose, 13, 15–16, 18, 22, 35, 42, 51

waste words: effect on syntax, 49, 56–58; obfuscation of meaning, 56; use together, 56–58, 61; *see also* "it," "that," "there," "this," "which"

"which," 60

WritersDiet Test: diagnosis of writing fitness, 2–3, 67; examples of, 16, 28, 38, 48, 62, 65, 70–71, 73; instructions for electronic version, 72; instructions for manual version, 68–69

zombie nouns, *see* nominalizations

Helen Sword is a Professor and Director of the Centre for Learning and Research in Higher Education at the University of Auckland. Trained as a literary scholar, she earned her PhD in Comparative Literature from Princeton University and taught for ten years in the English Department at Indiana University before taking up a lectureship in academic development at the University of Auckland in 2004. She has published widely on modernist literature, digital poetics, higher education pedagogy and academic writing, including five books – *Engendering Inspiration* (Michigan, 1995), *Ghostwriting Modernism* (Cornell, 2002), *The Writer's Diet* (first edition 2007), the co-edited volume *Pacific Rim Modernisms* (Toronto, 2009) and *Stylish Academic Writing* (Harvard, 2012) – and numerous scholarly articles and commentaries. In 2007 she was a co-recipient of the University of Auckland Teaching Excellence Award for Innovation in Teaching, and in 2013 she received the HERDSA-TERNZ Research Medal, awarded each year by the Higher Education Research and Development Society of Australasia. Sword's TED-Ed talk on "zombie nouns" has become a sleeper hit on YouTube, and she regularly offers workshops and seminars on stylish academic writing at universities around the world.